Three Minutes a Day

VOLUME 39

Other Christopher Books in Print

Better to Light One Candle
and other volumes in the
Three Minutes a Day
series

God Delights in You

Three Minutes a Day
Volume 39

Dennis Heaney
President, The Christophers

Stephanie Raha
Editor-in-Chief

Margaret O'Connell
Senior Research Editor

Staff Contributing Editors
Umberto Mignardi
Nicholas Monteleone
Regina Pappalardo
Anna Marie Tripodi

Contributors
Joan Bromfield
Monica Ann Yehle-Glick
Karen Hazel Radenbaugh
Anne Marie Welsh

Interns
Christine DelliBovi
Jennifer Hydicz
Katie Zajaczkowski
Melissa Kuch

The Christophers
12 East 48th Street
New York, NY 10017

Scriptural quotations in this publication are from the Revised Standard Version Bible, Catholic Edition, copyright 1965 and 1966 by the Division of Christian Education of the National Council of Churches of Christ in the U.S.A. and the New Revised Standard Version Bible, Catholic Edition, copyright 1989 by the Division of Christian Education of the National Council of Churches of Christ in the U.S.A. and used by permission.

If I speak in the tongues of mortals and of angels, but do not have love, I am a noisy gong or a clanging cymbal. And if I have prophetic powers, and understand all mysteries and all knowledge, and if I have all faith...but do not have love, I am nothing. If I give away all my possessions, and if I hand over my body so that I may boast, but do not have love, I gain nothing.

Love is patient; love is kind; love is not envious or boastful or arrogant or rude. It does not insist on its own way; it is not irritable or resentful; it does not rejoice in wrongdoing, but rejoices in the truth. It bears all things, believes all things, hopes all things, endures all things.

Love never ends. But as for prophecies, they will come to an end; as for tongues, they will cease; as for knowledge, it will come to an end. For we know only in part, and we prophesy only in part; but when the complete comes, the partial will come to an end. When I was a child, I spoke like a child, I thought like a child, I reasoned like a child; when I became an adult, I put an end to childish ways. For now we see in a mirror, dimly, but then we will see face to face. Now I know only in part; then I will know fully, even as I have been fully known. And now faith, hope, and love abide, these three; and the greatest of these is love.

1 CORINTHIANS 13

Introduction

"In these disturbing times there is a thrilling challenge in the realization that the world itself can be better because we are in it. ...We can, with Christ's help, actually help make this tired old world of ours the prelude to heaven! And since that is what God wants it to be, truly it is a great time to be alive. Now–and for all eternity–we can look with consolation on the part we have played...in shaping for the better the destiny of all!"

Father James Keller, M.M., wrote those stirring words in his book, *You Can Change the World!* not long after he founded The Christophers in 1945. As we celebrate our 60th anniversary in 2005, his words still ring true.

Our times are still disturbing. Violence, terrorism and war threaten us even as intolerance, fear and hatred create conflict around the globe.

But hope remains. As long as we use the gifts and opportunities God offers us not just for our own welfare, but for the good of all, we can meet the challenge.

If we choose to make a difference today and every day, we can say truthfully and enthusiastically, "It is a great time to be alive!"

And with God's blessing and your support, The Christophers will be encouraging new generations sixty years from now.

Dennis W. Heaney
President, The Christophers

Why be optimistic?

According to Dr. Martin Seligman at the University of Pennsylvania, success is more closely related to *how* people react to adversity than to their ability to *avoid* it.

He found that pessimists view failures as personal or inevitable and give up easily. Optimists, on the other hand, are more likely to persevere because they view failures as externally caused and only temporary. That perseverance means a greater success rate.

Dr. Seligman has also found that:

Optimism wins votes. Researchers were able to accurately predict the outcomes of elections depending on the optimism in candidates' speeches.

Optimism wins games. Baseball and basketball teams that talked optimistically to the press played better than those that talked pessimistically.

Optimism is healthier. After a first heart attack, more men who were optimistic survived than did those who were pessimistic.

Remember, optimism can be learned.

Hope does not disappoint us. (Romans 5:5)

Holy Spirit, fill me with optimism.

Raising the Bar

It's not unusual for Douglas Ammar to find himself in jail on any given day. As a Public Defender, his clients are the inmates in the crowded, noisy and tense Atlanta county jail.

Ammar enjoys his work. As the executive director of the Georgia Justice Project, he knows he is able to offer the toughest criminals from Atlanta's roughest neighborhoods a deal that's better for them—and for the public.

The Justice Project provides free legal representation to indigent Atlantans who sign a contract pledging to do whatever it takes to ensure that they never go back to jail again.

This effort to stem the recidivism rate—a form of legal 'tough love'—has worked. "The ones we have the most success with are usually the ones you'd think were the least ready to change their lives," says Ammar.

No effort at saving a human being is wasted. Each individual, no matter his or her situation, has worth and potential.

In this is love, not that we loved God but that He loved us and sent His Son to be the atoning sacrifice for our sins. (1 John 4:10)

Redeemer, reward efforts to help the troubled.

Desperately Needed: Clean Drinking Water

MIT-educated environmental engineer Susan Murcott is working to change the dreadful reality of a world desperately in need of clean drinking water.

About 2.2 million people, including children, die every year from drinking contaminated water. Many more get sick. For example, an estimated 25-70 million people in Bangladesh and half a million in Nepal suffer from arsenic poisoning. Found naturally in bedrock, the arsenic gets into drinking water from incorrectly placed wells.

Murcott and teams of graduate students are working on simple but creative solutions that families can use in their own homes. "Millions of people are suffering in ways that could be simply addressed," Murcott says. "For $5 a person, we could filter water for everyone across the globe."

Pure water shouldn't be a luxury. What can we do to help others enjoy what we too often take for granted?

The necessities of life are water, bread, and clothing, and also a house to assure privacy. (Sirach 29:21)

Help us appreciate the life-giving gift of water, Creator.

Lots of Cars, Not a Lot of Drivers

True or false: Most residents of New York City cannot drive. True. Only one in four New Yorkers actually possess a driver's license despite the over-crowded streets.

New Yorkers often plan work and play around their car-less reality. They work within subway or bus rides of their homes. They vacation in spots with good public transportation systems.

Besides, many would say that driving in New York is not natural. The city's Department of Transportation has measured the average speed of a car traveling in midtown Manhattan as approximately the rate of a Galapagos tortoise. And there are other problems: alternate side of the street parking, $100 parking tickets, high car insurance rates and pricey parking garages.

Still, life without wheels hasn't really stopped New Yorkers from being movers and shakers.

Nobody should make excuses for not being or doing all that they can.

The way of the lazy is overgrown with thorns, but the path of the upright is a level highway. (Proverbs 15:19)

Help me make a difference today, Lord. May one person feel Your love through my actions.

Thriving Through Life

Dr. Bill Thomas wrote a fable–and then made it real. In *Learning from Hannah: Secrets for a Life Worth Living*, Thomas imagines that he and his wife are shipwrecked on a mysterious island called Kallimos. There older residents are embraced by the younger generations who value their wisdom and experience. Inspired by Hannah, their mentor on the island, the Thomases return to civilization and start Eden Alternative.

In the real world Thomas appeared on radio and television, and met with public officials to discuss the flaws of nursing homes–no hope, no love, no humor, no meaning. The gerontologist spoke of needed changes: adding pets and plants; welcoming children; nurturing relationships between caregivers and residents.

"People are meant to live in a garden, a place where they can grow and thrive," says Thomas.

Traveling along life's road means taking time to stop and plant the roses!

Gray hair is a crown of glory; it is gained in a righteous life. (Proverbs 16:31)

Nurture Your life within me, Lord. May my actions praise You all my days!

Creativity in the Workplace

Good business managers know it takes more than a paycheck to help employees be productive. Sometimes it means recognizing that workers are people first, then adding a little innovation.

Knowing that individuals who are sleep-deprived are less productive, one consulting firm put reclining chairs and blankets in a quiet room for staff members who needed a quick nap. Another company permitted workers to shop on-line during their lunch hours and breaks, and even installed a couple of high-speed terminals to help them finish their personal tasks. One large corporation set up employee resource groups to offer suggestions. A number of their ideas were implemented, including a childcare center.

Seeing people as individuals is as crucial at home and in your community as it is on the job. Open your eyes, your mind and your heart to those around you.

Clothe yourselves with compassion, kindness. (Colossians 3:12)

Holy God, You gave me a body, a brain and a soul—and the chance to use them well each day. Guide my efforts to do good.

Scientist Has Hope

"I feel deep shame when I look into the eyes of my grandchildren and think how much damage has been done to Planet Earth since I was their age," writes scientist Jane Goodall. "Each of us must work as hard as we can now to save what is left."

Goodall sets a fine example. Through partnerships with environmentally conscious companies around the world, she has initiated reforestation projects and established educational programs.

She is quick to acknowledge that people can feel helpless in the face of a task as enormous as saving the planet. "You are just one person in a world of six billion," she says. "How can your actions make a difference?"

But she believes that it's possible to overcome apathy with hope: "I derive the most hope from the energy and hard work of young people."

Have hope. No matter how tough life gets. Have hope.

Set an example. (Judith 8:24)

Help us commit to the right path, God, mindful that others will follow.

A Little House in England

Outside, the house is unremarkable, typical of 1930s England. Inside it's the 1950s: the kitchen has checkered linoleum and floral print porcelain; aquamarine and cream-colored cabinets; a retractable clothesline for dishtowels; and a tin box with the word "bread" stenciled on the side.

A bedroom upstairs has a few posters, including one of Elvis Presley. Forty-fives (vinyl records) by Little Richard and Lonnie Donegan have been carefully strewn around the room to give the appearance that its former occupant is still living there.

The restoration of the house where Beatle John Lennon lived with his aunt and uncle from 1945 to 1963 was completed by the National Trust in 2003. His widow says she was really touched when she first saw the tiny bedroom. "Somehow he made an incredible dream go out from there, a dream shared by the whole world," remarked Yoko Ono.

Mine the depths of your God-given talents. The world will be richer.

Be strongly encouraged to seize the hope set before us. (Hebrews 6:18)

Loving Spirit, never let our circumstances prevent us from big dreams and bigger accomplishments.

A Commitment to Compassion

"What kind of society are we if we turn our backs on those who need help most?"

That's what Dr. Pedro Jose Greer, Jr., wants to know. Greer, the volunteer medical director at the Camillus Health Concern Clinic in Miami, has treated the homeless and uninsured in his community for more than 20 years. He is also chief of gastroenterology at Miami's Mercy Hospital, and known for taking on politicians, insurance executives and hospital administrators in an effort to improve healthcare for all people.

Dr. Greer has encouraged medical schools to include clinics among the rotations their students make; he has brought young doctors with him on his rounds with the homeless. Nationwide, programs in 20 cities follow his lead.

"It may sound idealistic, but it's true: With kindness and compassion, we really can make the world a better place," says Dr. Greer.

Kindness and compassion can change everything.

Give graciously to all the living; do not withhold kindness even from the dead. Do not avoid those who weep...visit the sick. (Sirach 7:33-34,35)

Divine Physician, forgive us our judgmental attitudes toward the sick, the poor and the homeless. Open our hearts to love.

Bringing Families Closer

Barbara Fiese, Ph.D., chair and professor of psychology at Syracuse University, says that small, thoughtful habits promote a feeling of security and love between people. She calls them "the shorthand of communication."

Some examples of little things that work:

When one couple eats out, he spoons his croutons onto her plate, winking as he does it.

Another husband and wife expect that every Sunday morning their pre-teen children will join them for cuddle time.

At supper, parents ask their children to talk about the best and worst parts of the day just past, as well as their hopes for the next day.

A couple sit together over wine or tea for one hour each evening, focusing on only each other. Dinner comes later.

The divorced orthodox Jewish father of teens blesses his children and at Sabbath meals turns the conversation to life, religion and future hopes.

What rituals are important to you and your loved ones?

Every year His parents went to Jerusalem for the festival of the Passover. (Luke 2:41-42)

Redeemer, bless relationships with small kindnesses and genuine communication.

"The most important work I could do"

"Please don't hang up. You needn't say anything more, I'm just afraid of being alone," the woman said to the Lifeline volunteer counselor.

Thirty years ago Rev. Yukio Saito, a Methodist minister, opened Lifeline, a suicide hotline, in Japan. He had become "convinced...that saving lives was the most important work I could do," and wanted to persuade the isolated and despondent to live.

Then, there was a single telephone bank. Now there are 50 call-in centers, most operating 24 hours a day, with over 7,000 volunteer counselors. Their "job is to understand...to accept the feelings" of those who call and to offer company to the lonely.

In Japan and elsewhere, families spend little time together. Friends socialize via the internet or telephone. The aged and sick are often alone. Rev. Saito says, "Loneliness has become universal."

We have all known what it's like to be alone–and afraid of being alone. Reach out to others. Communicate. Socialize.

Two...if they fall, one will lift up the other...if two lie together, they keep warm...two will withstand one. (Ecclesiastes 4:9,10,11,12)

Jesus, who felt forsaken by Your Father, help us ease others' loneliness and so our own.

Through New Eyes

When Geoffrey Bardon was 30-years old, the elementary school teacher and artist was assigned to work in Papunya in central Australia, an area so remote it wasn't on maps.

He learned the language of the Papunya's Aboriginal inhabitants and worked hard to gain the trust of his students and their parents. Observing that Papunya was "a community in distress, oppressed by exile, and a place of emotional loss and waste," he still recognized the importance of the local artwork.

Donating paints and brushes, he encouraged the people of Papunya to work on canvas. He then helped them bring their unique, indigenous art to the attention of the world by forming a cooperative. Through his efforts, Bardon kindled a revival of Papunyan art that has led to films, exhibits, books, and worldwide attention.

What can you do to encourage others' creativity?

Encourage one another. (1 Thessalonians 4:18)

May my talents encourage those most in need, Lord.

Silver and Gold

Wanting to know how people would describe their friends and the importance of friendship, *Family Circle* magazine asked several women what they thought:

- Dancer-choreographer Nicole Barth, who has been friends with actress Valerie Harper for more than four decades: "she's reliable. She's there no matter what–a very steady, very humorous force… a safe comfort zone…a rock."

- Newswoman Meredith Vieira, who has enjoyed her 22-year friendship with Mo Cashin, unit manager at CBS: "her great sense of humor… listening…very forgiving."

If reliability, safety, comfortableness, humor, listening, forgiving describe our everyday friends, how much more Jesus? Joseph Scriven knew what he was talking about when he wrote the hymn, *What a Friend We Have in Jesus.*

A true friend sticks closer than one's nearest kin. (Proverbs 18:24)

What a privilege to carry everything to You in prayer, Divine Friend.

Reviving a Long-Lost Practice

In 1940, 40 percent of doctors made house calls: today, one percent.

Dr. Donald Rumbaugh carries the traditional black leather bag up the steps of many of his patients' homes for house calls. The middle-aged Rumbaugh is one of a handful of doctors who have revived the house call in recent years.

"I noticed some people were too sick to come and see me, and they needed medical care desperately," he says. "I bring my charts and my gear, and I go to them."

Sometimes what's new and newfangled isn't always best. There is wisdom in time-honored past traditions.

There may come a time when recovery lies in the hands of physicians, for they too pray to the Lord that He grant them success in diagnosis and in healing, for the sake of preserving life. (Sirach 38:13).

God, help me avoid fads and trends. Help me keep my focus on what really matters, no matter how simple.

Facing the Past

"Dad told us never to go in there," said Isaac Lang, Jr., 84, from his nursing home bed. "He said, 'Boys, I'm going to tell you the truth. It's all right to play around that barn, but don't go inside'. He said it just wasn't right. That it was pitiful. He never did tell us why."

The painful truth was that this particular Kentucky tobacco barn concealed a slave jail where Capt. John W. Anderson, a slave trader, had kept countless enslaved African-Americans in the first half of the nineteenth century. It's been authenticated as one of the few remains of the time when America had a network of holding pens, jails and yards for slaves. It is slated to become part of Cincinnati's National Underground Railroad Freedom Center.

Many would like to forget, ignore or bury history. Others understand that the past must be remembered. As individuals or as a nation, only by confronting the past can we begin healing the present.

Those who despise their neighbors are sinners. (Proverbs 14:21)

God, help us face up to our past and to forgive or to make amends.

On E-mail Etiquette

Over the last few years people have learned that e-mail offers lots of pluses and some major minuses.

Errors, missed messages and wasted time can result from the poor use of e-mail. Businesses have also discovered that many workers rely on it so much that they lose face-to-face contact with one another, actually isolating themselves from the normal give-and-take of office life.

That's why Richard Foos, co-founder of Rhino Entertainment, decided to ban employee-to-employee e-mail. While they can send as many messages to people outside the company as they want, workers at the Los Angeles company are expected to get up from their desks and talk with their coworkers.

Convenience, in whatever form, can be a boon. But human relationships matter. Hiding behind a screen or a stack of work or a self-centered attitude doesn't help; getting to know and respect one another does. Next time you want to share a message, deliver it in person.

Pleasant speech multiplies friends. (Sirach 6:5)

Holy God, why do we hide from relationships? You love us as individuals. Open our hearts and minds to each other.

Meaning of Courage

Dr. Martin Luther King, Jr., put himself on the line for the human rights of others to the point of laying down his own life. Here's what he had to say about both courage and cowardice:

"Courage and cowardice are antithetical. Courage is an inner resolution to go forward in spite of obstacles and frightening situations; cowardice is a submissive surrender to circumstance. Courage breeds creative self-affirmation; cowardice produces destructive self-abnegation. Courage faces fear and thereby masters it.

"Courageous persons never lose the zest for living even though their life situation is zestless; cowards, overwhelmed by the uncertainties of life, lose the will to live. We must constantly build dykes of courage to hold back the flood of fear."

We tend to think we only need courage to deal with life's great problems. In truth, we need to be brave each day—or we will never be brave when we must.

No one has greater love than this, to lay down one's life for one's friends. (John 15:13)

Touch my mind and my heart, Holy Spirit, and show me how to be brave each hour of my life so that I may better serve You.

A Sense of Village

Reed Karaim and his family loved living in Fairlington, just outside of Washington, DC. It was like living in a village.

The area actually started out in the 1940s as housing for workers at the Pentagon, with townhouses and apartment buildings laid out to conform to the land. Tree-lined streets dotted with gardens add to the homey feel. Today families still stroll the neighborhood and throw potluck suppers for each other.

The Karaim family came to embrace not only a sense of neighborliness, but also a sense of shared responsibility. Then, Karaim's wife accepted a position with the University of Arizona. They moved out west and not only had to choose a new home but also a new neighborhood. But Karaim felt the Fairlington experience would help them in their new community.

Wherever you live, contribute to neighborliness and to tolerance.

When (Jesus) came to Nazareth, where He had been brought up, He went to the synagogue on the Sabbath day, as was His custom. (Luke 4:16)

Remind us how interdependent we are, God our Creator and Sustainer.

A Mystery Evermore

For 54 years, an unknown man has crept into a Baltimore graveyard early on a mid-January morning to toast the memory and legacy of Edgar Allan Poe. Hidden under a dark hood, the man leaves red roses and a bottle of cognac on the grave before fading back into the pre-dawn shadows.

Jeff Jerome, curator of the Poe House and Museum, and other Poe aficionados have watched this annual ritual from a nearby church since 1976. "It would be very easy to step out...and expose him, but no one wants to end this mystery."

Many of us enjoy unraveling a good mystery, but some of life's little mysteries are better appreciated unsolved. Albert Einstein once said, "The most beautiful experience we can have is the mysterious."

When was the last time you enjoyed life as it is, instead of seeing it as a problem to be solved?

When Israel went out from Egypt...The sea looked and fled; Jordan turned back. The mountains skipped like rams, the hills like lambs. (Psalm 114:1,3-4)

Lord, help us to value the mystery in this world.

No Greater Gift

In the highly competitive world of athletics, Esther Kim displayed an inspiring act of selflessness.

Kim, 20, and her best friend Kay Poe, 18, both black belts in tae kwon do, faced each other in a match to see who would land a spot on the U.S. Olympic team bound for Sydney, Australia.

The young women approached the mat, bowed and faced the referee. But before the fight could commence, the referee awarded the match to Poe. Kim had forfeited it. Why?

For Esther Kim, it seemed the right thing to do. She knew her friend Kay was about to fight despite having a badly swollen dislocated kneecap, injured in an earlier semifinal match.

"It wasn't fair for me to go in there having two legs and her having only one," said Kim.

Her proud father told her "You are a true champion, a champion of life. You did this for a friend."

Deal courageously, and may the Lord be with the good. (2 Chronicles 19:11)

Help us, Lord, to make courageous decisions.

Mush for the Cure

On January 21, 1925, Dr. Curtis Welch first diagnosed a diphtheria outbreak in Nome, Alaska. An antitoxin existed for the disease, but Dr. Welch only had enough for five patients. With Nome's port frozen until spring and the only available planes over 500 miles away in Fairbanks–where they had already been dismantled and put into winter storage–the outlook was dire.

Dr. Welch sent telegraph messages to cities around Alaska asking for help. A physician in Anchorage shipped the only available serum via train to the town closest to Nome, 674 miles away.

Then, with the help of the Northern Commercial Company and the Army Signal Corps, twenty men and more than 150 sled dogs relayed the cylinder across Alaska's frozen interior, fighting gales of over 80 miles per hour as well as sub-zero temperatures. Dr. Welch lifted the quarantine one month later.

Many working together saved hundreds of lives that January. What will you do next time someone asks for your help?

We know love by this, that He laid down His life for us–and we ought to lay down our lives for one another...love...in truth and action. (1 John 3:16,18)

Father, enable us to willingly go to the aid of those in need.

Small Town Success

Growing up in a small town, Peggy Conlon valued her mother's generosity, including housing and feeding another family. But Conlon felt her mother had missed something by never leaving the tiny town.

Conlon moved to New York City, but after a decade of financial success, began to realize it was she, not her mother, who was missing something.

Then she saw an opening for president of the Ad Council, a nonprofit organization which raises awareness about major social issues. "I saw it as a chance to do something with meaning," said Conlon. She got the job.

Soon after her mother died, Conlon headed a campaign in honor of her mother. "It became important for me to campaign against child hunger."

No matter where you live, you, too, could be missing something. Be open to finding that something in your life.

His favor brings lasting success. (Sirach 11:17)

Holy Spirit, help me find eternal and enduring meaning in work and in life.

Flower Power

"Making art...gets you to want to live, it appeals to the part of the brain where imagination lies," says Bill Strickland, a Pittsburgh entrepreneur.

Strickland's imagination was ignited when a dinner guest gave him a deep-purple orchid. A trip to the Zuma Canyon Orchids greenhouse in Malibu, California followed.

Discovering that orchids "are dramatic and colorful, but...evoke powerful feelings of contemplation and peace," Strickland decided to raise $3.5 million to build an orchid greenhouse in his own inner city Manchester neighborhood. It took seven years.

The 46,000-square-foot greenhouse opened in February, 2003. Five high school graduates who weren't going to college were among the first hires. Says Zuma Canyon Orchids' owner George Vazquez, "By showing these (inner-city kids) that they can grow something luxurious, Bill (Strickland) is telling them they have self-worth."

Tell someone that they have self-worth. Save a life.

You are precious in my sight, and honored, and I love you. (Isaiah 43:4)

Remind us, Jesus, that You love each one of us individually, personally, passionately.

Visiting a Sick Friend

Many of us grew up with the idea that visiting the sick is a work of mercy. Yet, doing it in a kind, useful way takes more than showing up at the door of an ill neighbor. Here are some tips:

- Call before you visit and when you get there, keep it short. Be alert to the patient's signs of fatigue.

- Listen to the patient. Touch him or her gently. Be positive without false cheeriness. Avoid criticizing the treatment.

- Offer help to the patient and family—run an errand, baby-sit, etc.—whatever they really need, not what seems right to you.

- After the visit, stay in touch. Send cards, call and if the illness is prolonged, visit again.

- Remember to pray.

Above all, treat the patient as a person, not an illness. That way, this work of mercy can be a real gift of love.

Come, you that are blessed by My Father, inherit the kingdom...(for) I was sick and you took care of Me. (Matthew 25:34,36)

Dear Father, bless Your wounded children with healing and bless their caregivers as well.

Riding God's Plan

Bethany Hamilton is a brave and thankful young woman. The thirteen-year old miraculously survived a shark attack while drifting on her surfboard off a Hawaiian beach. A tiger shark bit off her left arm, possibly ending the teenager's budding pro-surfing career. Despite all this, Bethany is staying positive and focused on the future.

"There's no time machine," she said. "I can't change it. That was God's plan for my life, and I'm going to go with it."

And the teen certainly is going with it. While in the hospital, Bethany visited a young patient suffering from a brain tumor and a blind man, offering support and helping to lift their spirits. She's determined not only to help others but to return to her championship surfing form.

God's plan for us may not always lead us through familiar waters. Go with it, and know that you are not alone.

The Lord went in front of them in a pillar of cloud by day...and in a pillar of fire by night. (Exodus 13:21)

Father, help me make Your will my will.

A Simpler Time

In a world constantly tearing down and building anew, some folks are stepping back in time to the Old West.

Homeowners in New Mexico and Montana are repairing the homes of early pioneers. Marsha Perkins, for example, passed up buying a condo to rebuild a crumbling century-old ranch house. "I wanted this house—it's really a reminder of the tenacity of the people who came here to put up with all the elements," Perkins said.

September 11th contributed to this trend as busy urban dwellers hoped to return to a simpler and supposedly safer time and place. Bernie Weisgerber, a historic preservation specialist, said, "life is just too fast-paced now."

By restoring or rebuilding old houses, these homeowners are suggesting that new is not always better. Take time to remember and to celebrate the courage of those who have gone before us.

**Hard work was created for everyone.
(Sirach 40:1)**

Thank you, Lord, for helping our ancestors persevere. Bless us with that same strength today.

Praise and Encouragement

For decades, Fred "Mr." Rogers closed his daily show by reminding children that "you made this day special just by being yourself." He conveyed to others the same sense of importance and uniqueness that was given to him as a boy.

Fred Rogers's Grandfather McFeely had told him as a boy, "Remember, there's only one person in this whole world like you, and I like you exactly as you are."

Being a grandparent offers precious opportunities to instill self-esteem in a child. Your love, your words and your care have a tremendous and life-long impact on your grandchildren.

Grandchildren are the crown of the aged. (Proverbs 17:6)

God, bless the elderly. Remind them of their value and importance in the lives of those around them. And grant them the energy and enthusiasm to live each day fully.

Curious Origins

Ever wonder about some of the common food-oriented phrases we use, and where they come from? The English language is full of odd terms that often have their origins in surprisingly literal circumstances.

During the Middle Ages, for example, it was common to *give a cold shoulder* of beef to guests who had overstayed their welcome as a hint that it was time to leave. Low-grade minstrels who couldn't afford cold cream would use *ham* fat to remove their makeup, sparking the term that would become synonymous with overacting. In Britain, married couples could *bring home the bacon* by winning it in a church-sponsored competition. And *stewing in one's own juices* took the idea of suffering consequences to an extreme in the 13th century: it was a euphemism for being burned at the stake.

There is so much remarkable information that can be ours with some reading and research. Stay interested and involved in the larger world.

Their children spoke...the language of various peoples. (Nehemiah 13:24)

Lord, help us to investigate the world around us.

Coping With Grief

Reaching out to others can help to heal grief. After her teenage son was accidentally electrocuted, Peggy Myrick went into a tailspin of misery, drinking heavily and eventually divorcing as the unbearable tragedy strained her marriage.

But ten years after Gary's death, Myrick says that she "found redemption in the form of a miniature horse named Freddy Stallion." Now she runs a petting zoo.

The Springville, California, native became something of a local Pied Piper as she took Freddy Stallion on daily walks through town followed by happy youngsters, many from broken homes.

She tells of one girl so overjoyed that she was in tears after riding Freddy for the first time. Peggy Myrick says, "These kids were so used to not having anything. She was so happy to be riding a pony on her twelfth birthday."

Do all you can to ease the burdens of those around us.

Do not give your heart to grief...you do the dead no good, and you injure yourself. (Sirach 38:20,21)

God, may we learn to heal our own sorrow by bringing joy to others.

Becoming a "Thriver"

What's the difference between surviving and thriving?

Psychologist Paul Pearsall, Ph.D., offers this insight: "Surviving is unrelenting perseverance that brings us back to where we were before a crisis. Thriving is a kind of super-resilience that goes beyond recovery."

Pearsall believes thrivers know when, for example, it's time to disengage from a challenge and set new goals. Thrivers also turn suffering to their advantage by adopting a more deeply appreciative and energized involvement in daily living.

Thrivers are able, says Pearsall, "to laugh in the face of their adversity, to argue effectively against their own negative and self-defeating thoughts, and to find something positive about their situation."

In short, surviving is coping; thriving, creating.

Endure with patience. (Baruch 4:25)

Lord, bless us with a new vision for creatively managing our lives, so that we may rise above difficulties and turn them into something positive.

A Guardian Angel

At the end of the school day, third graders Melanie Lonzano and Amy Romo were waiting in a classroom for Amy's parents who worked in the school. Amy's three-year-old sister, Gabriella, or Gabby, who was with them, was happily munching a peppermint candy when she suddenly began choking.

Melanie had learned the Heimlich maneuver as a Girl Scout Brownie. So she threw her arms around Gabby's waist and gave a quick firm squeeze. The candy popped out of Gabby's mouth and she gasped for air.

By then Gabby's stunned parents had arrived and were praising Melanie as a "guardian angel." Melanie had learned more than just a life-saving maneuver as a Brownie; she had also developed a spirit of helpfulness.

It's never too early or too late to learn.

The Most High...will command His angels...to guard you in all your ways. (Psalm 91:9,11)

God, give me patience and perseverance as I try to do Your work.

Ordinary People, Extraordinary Changes

Think you and your friends can't make a difference? Think again.

"Four guys met, planned, and went into action," said Franklin McCain. "It's just that simple." And America would never be the same.

In 1960 McCain and three other students at the all-black North Carolina Agricultural and Technical College in Greensboro decided to put an end to the racial discrimination that plagued black people every day. So they dared to take seats at a "whites only" lunch counter. This simple action initiated a vital chapter in the civil rights movement.

Though much has improved, not all hatred, discrimination and intolerance have disappeared. The struggle for justice and equality is ongoing. By getting involved and working together, we can help insure the civil rights of all.

Think about that the next time you join your friends for lunch.

Those who do not love a brother or sister whom they have seen can not love God whom they have not seen. (1 John 4:20)

Lord, give success to our struggles against hatred, discrimination and intolerance.

All in the Family

Corey and Millicent Bell had a good life. Married and working for Dell Computer, they had moved into a new five-bedroom house in a golf club community. Kids? Well, they'd come sometime down the line. Everything had been planned and perfect, until Corey's mother–a single mom–died.

Corey is the oldest of 13 children and his mother's death left eight of his siblings, aged 7 to 18, at home and in need of care. After much debate and prayer, the Bells decided to take in the orphaned brothers and sisters, thus expanding their family of two to one of ten.

"We just want to give the kids a better life," Corey says. "They may never...understand the sacrifice...They just need to know it's a better life."

Each of us has so much to offer to ensure a "better life" for all. What would you do for the ones you love?

Love deeply from the heart. (1 Peter 1:22)

Jesus, You made the ultimate sacrifice for us. Thank You.

Re-imagining Our Heroes

"Where have all the heroes gone?" laments *The Royal Bank (of Canada) Letter.* Despite a wariness about losing its own culture to that of its superpower neighbor, studies show that young Canadians know more about Davy Crockett than about explorers like the LeMoyne brothers who helped explore Canada's frontier.

In the case of Davy Crockett, the reason may be a once popular television program. Still, it may be time for all of us to redefine our notion of heroism.

What are today's real heroes doing? They are battling violence and poverty, disease and hunger, inhumanity and injustice, mostly anonymously.

And the *Royal Bank Letter* makes a good point when it adds, "If parents find their children have no wholesome role models, then they must strive to become those role models themselves."

Be a role model, a hero–in your own way.

The measure you give will be the measure you get. (Mark 4:24)

God, deepen our hunger for authenticity in our lives.

Dogged Determination to Help

Pamela Atkinson has been literally reaching out to Salt Lake City's homeless for 17 years. "When you shake a homeless person's hand, it might be the only time they are touched that week."

Naturally her commitment goes beyond a handshake. Many people count on her practical assistance which includes providing food, blankets and access to medical care.

She has even been known to help out a pet or two. "For some homeless people, love from a pet is the only love they get," she explains. So there are always a few bags of dog food in the trunk of her car.

She once paid for an operation on a dog that had been run over. As the owner thanked her, he explained that she had saved two lives: "I couldn't have lived without Skip. He's all I have."

There are so many ways to reach out. Explore some of them soon.

Let us test and examine our ways, and return to the Lord. (Lamentations 3:40)

Expand our hearts and minds, O Lord, to see things from Your perspective.

Self Improvement through Reading

Reading for pleasure. Reading for information. Reading for adventure. And, yes, reading for enlightenment.

All reading isn't the same and need not be. Writing about literacy in the *New York Times*, Edward Rothstein says there was a time when people read for enlightenment without feeling either embarrassment or shame.

"But what if snobbery and shame are both misplaced? What if preferences for the high achievements of culture were not expressed with snobbery but with advocacy that ignored social class?

"And what if the shame were undercut by the recognition that such preferences are not, in themselves, inconsistent with democratic ideals?"

So read those magazines and bestsellers. But make time for "Moby Dick" and Boswell's "Life of Johnson," too. There's a reason they're called great books. Indulge yourself and encourage your loved ones to do the same.

Jesus...returned to Galilee, and...went to the synagogue on the Sabbath day, as was His custom. He stood up to read. (Luke 4:1,16)

Holy Spirit, inspire us to keep learning and growing.

People, Ya Gotta Love 'Em

A sign at a café in Menlo Park, California, presented some interesting thoughts about human nature. Here are a few:

"People are...unreasonable, illogical, self-centered.

"People will accuse you of ulterior motives.

"People (will) favor underdogs but follow only topdogs.

"Give the world the best you've got."

"Be honest and frank" though you are vulnerable.

"Do good though it will be forgotten tomorrow."

And be successful. Why? Because to be honest, frank, good and successful is to become the real you; the you God created you to be.

Think: if each person lived this positive way, the world would be a better place faster than anyone would ever think possible.

None...will lose their reward. (Matthew 10:42)

Becoming the person You created me to be is challenging, Abba. Help me.

Come Again?

Here's a conversation recently overheard at a bagel vendor's cart in New York City:

"Can I have a cinnamon raisin with nothing?"

"I only have cinnamon raisin with something... and sesame with something... also, poppy with something."

"Don't you have anything with nothing?"

"The only thing I have with nothing is an everything."

(FYI: "everything" bagels have poppy and sesame seeds, salt and other toppings; and "something" is butter or cream cheese.)

Laughing at life's little absurdities can make any day more enjoyable. Keep an open eye and ear, and enjoy them.

By the way, the customer bought a muffin instead.

For everything there is a season, and a time for every matter under heaven...a time to laugh...a time to dance. (Ecclesiastes 3:1,4)

Lord, help us to enjoy all life has to offer.

Clowns Aren't Just for Kids

When Esther Gushner, also known as Dr. CurlyBubbe, walks into a hospital room, patients can't help but get in on the fun. Gushner is one of 29 people who make up the Bumper "T" Caring Clowns. These volunteers visit adult patients to "bring out the kid" in them.

The Caring Clowns serve seven hospitals in the southern New Jersey and Philadelphia area. They continue to train more people to spread smiles through the program.

"Becoming a Caring Clown will add a special dimension to the care we provide," said Alice Malfi of ACMC (Atlantic City Medical Center). "Patients of all ages can benefit from the touch of happiness clowns deliver."

"At the end of the day, you've bagged hundreds of smiles," says Gushner. "It really puts your life in perspective because you realize how lucky you are."

Spread joy whenever you can.

Rejoicing lengthens one's life span. ...Remove sorrow far from you. (Sirach 30:22, 23)

Help me bring joy to those who are in need of it the most, Lord.

A Life of Prayer

When He wanted to pray, Jesus would often "withdraw to deserted places" (Luke 5:16) or go "out to the mountain" to spend "the night in prayer." (Luke 6:12)

Jesus also suggested to others that they "shut the door" to one's room and "pray to your Father...in secret." (Matthew 6:6)

Almost two thousand years later, the great human rights activist and political leader Mohandas Gandhi defined prayer as: "The key to the morning, the lock of the evening...a sacred alliance between God and man."

Gandhi believed that prayer saved his life and his mind. He noted the peace that comes from prayer. And Gandhi wrote, "we can live for a few days without eating, but not without praying."

Would you define prayer as your soul's food or your life-saver, your alliance with God?

Develop your prayer life. You might try praying from Jesus' own prayer book, The Psalms.

Let my prayer be counted as incense before You, and the lifting up of my hands as an evening sacrifice. (Psalm 141:2)

Abba, O Father, teach me to search for my personal prayer style.

A Bright Spot

Veronica Smith used to spend her weeks waiting for Thursdays. It was then she would snuggle and play with her infant daughter, Kaydonna, for two hours in the chapel of the Kentucky prison where she was incarcerated.

The rest of the time Kaydonna lived at Angel House, which was started by Sandy Tucker and her husband, Jerry. They have cared for more than 400 children and babies of women in prison, so that the state would not have to take custody of them. The children enjoy a cheerful, homey, family-like atmosphere and the opportunity to see their moms. Their moms in turn are happy knowing that when they leave prison, their children will be waiting.

"It's a reason (for the mothers) to straighten out their lives, a light at the end of the tunnel," says Sandy.

Our world is full of ways to help neighbors. Find yours.

Do not despise one of these little ones; for I tell you, in heaven their angels continually see the face of My Father. (Matthew 18:10)

Show us new ways to fix the brokenness in our lives and the lives of those we meet, Lord.

Hoping for the Best

Sheila Cassidy credits Benedictine monk Tom Cullinan for teaching her that hope must be distinguished from expectation.

Cullinan told her that expectation is what, given the circumstances, is likely to happen, whereas hope is the knowledge that God can always bring good out of evil, light out of darkness, life out of death.

This definition resonated with Cassidy's personal and professional experiences. She is a palliative care expert working with terminally ill people.

"Hope is a hot potato in the world of cancer patients and their families. Patients cling to it like a life raft," she says.

She finds this image particularly powerful in the face of despair: "Hope is not the hands which build the house. Hope is the hands which shape the rubble into some kind of a shelter for the night when the house is ruined."

Good can come out of evil, if we trust God and ourselves to make it so.

There is a reward for your work, says the Lord. (Jeremiah 31:16)

Be our true hope, loving God.

Living Large on Less

Reducing spending is an unwelcome but often necessary part of our adult lives. But what happens if you've cut all the corners you can, but still can't make ends meet? Fortunately, there may still be ways to save by changing your lifestyle.

Start by eliminating all entertainment that costs money. Visit art galleries and museums on their free nights. Usher at concerts. Support local artists by attending open-mike nights. Videos and books borrowed from your local public library are other sources of free entertainment.

Brew coffee and tea at home rather than buying drinks at coffeehouses. Avoid meters by parking your car farther away and walking. Rediscover the clothesline rather than using a dryer.

Resourcefulness is a great ally in times of scarcity. How can you use your creativity to work through life's difficulties?

Do not revel in great luxury, or you may become impoverished by its expense. (Sirach 18:32)

God, grant me the strength and perseverance to find creative solutions to the challenges I face.

Real Men Speak Out

Gloucester, Massachusetts, knew it had a problem with domestic violence. The local battered women's center was often crowded with frightened women and children, clinging to one another for support.

To stem the tide of violence, the community also knew it had to get men involved. First, the city declared itself a domestic violence-free zone, and 550 Gloucester men sent the town's women a Valentine's Day card: a billboard bearing their names and saying "Strong Men Don't Bully."

Other efforts followed, all to gather the support of the men of the community, not just the women, in the fight against domestic abuse. "Men have 'permission' from the male community to express concern about these issues," says one community activist.

Since so-called "women-oriented" issues affect everyone, men have a vital role in working to end domestic violence.

Put away violence and oppression, and do what is just and right. (Ezekiel 45:9)

Jesus, protect women and men throughout the world, as they work against discrimination, injustice and psychological, sexual and physical abuse.

Forgiveness at Home

Remember the saying, "Charity begins at home"? Well, so does forgiveness. We can't expect to pardon strangers who hurt us in ways large or small, if we do not practice forgiveness within our family circle.

Dietrich Bonhoeffer, the renowned Lutheran pastor and theologian who was murdered by the Nazis for his resistance activities, believed strongly in the importance of forgiveness, starting with married couples. In "A Wedding Sermon," he wrote: "Live together in the forgiveness of your sins for without it, no human fellowship...can survive. Don't insist on your rights, don't blame each other, don't judge or condemn each other, don't find fault with each other, but take one another as you are, and forgive each other every day from the bottom of your heart."

Forgiveness never means accepting abuse, but it does mean allowing for the everyday failures and follies of human nature. Forgive others. Forgive yourself. And get on with your life.

One who forgives an affront fosters friendship. (Proverbs 17:9)

Holy Lord, I beg Your pardon for my sins, for the evil I've done, for the good I've left undone. And help me to forgive all who injure me.

Life on the Line

Crisis hotline volunteer Sherry Amathenstein found herself connected to a caller contemplating suicide.

The woman told Amathenstein that her parents had disowned her; two accidents had left her in pain and unable to work; her fiancé had died of cancer. "Give me a reason to live," the caller challenged.

"How could I summon the words to give someone else's life meaning?" thought Amathenstein, who concluded that she must "help her fan the spark that had led her to reach out." They spoke and prayed for hours. Finally the woman said, "I think I'll be all right for the night."

"As I hung up, I realized the call had meant as much to me as to her, if not more," said the volunteer. "Instead of having dinner at an over-priced restaurant or watching television, I'd connected with another soul."

Where there is life, there is always an opportunity to reach out in hope.

Guard my life, and deliver me. (Psalm 25:20)

In my darkest hour, Lord, You are my hope; my strength.

Want a Happier Life? Then Make One!

Some believe happiness is something that happens by luck of the draw—some people get it, some don't. But research suggests otherwise.

Parents, for example, can greatly increase the chances that their children will grow up to be happy, responsible adults by instilling in them optimism, playfulness, a can-do attitude and an overall sense of emotional security. As one psychologist says, "Happiness is something you can make happen."

Many situations in life are beyond our control. Others call for our direct involvement and efforts. When it comes to happiness, your attitude and outlook are crucial.

How can you become a happier person?

**Rejoice in the happiness of a friend.
(Sirach 37:4)**

God, give me the wisdom to accept what I can not change, the courage to change what I can.

A Beast Fable

Writing in *The Word* magazine Noel Martin imagines an Earth ruled by the Creatures. Here are excerpts from his poem:

"No food would rot in storage/Whilst millions starve and die/...An earth free from pollution/...Our seas, clear, and unpoisoned..."

Martin concludes "If people were as faithful/As the average family pet/Industrious, as ants and bees/What bounty to beget/...no begrudgement/Nor jealousy or hate/Just...love, and sharing/Should animals dictate."

Pollyannish? Maybe. Maybe not. Think—only humans can pollute and drain rivers, wells and acquifers; blow up mountains for ore and coal; develop and dump heavy metals and poisonous chemicals; exploit workers; abuse children and the elderly; judge the poor harshly.

Be idealistic; be tender, loving, faithful, industrious, sharing and caring of all people, all creatures, God's Good Earth.

It is required of stewards that they be found trustworthy. (1 Corinthians 4:2)

Creator, give us the courage to live in justice and harmony with all the living.

Much Needed Parts

Having a good idea is one thing. Getting others to go along with it is quite another.

A few years ago, Gordon Bethune, President and CEO of Continental Airlines, wanted to improve the company's on-time record. He offered a $65 bonus to every employee for each month that they ranked among the top five. Within just two months they soared from last place to first.

That's when some workers complained that since not everyone's job affected on-time performance, they shouldn't be included in the bonus plan. At a meeting, Bethune held up his wristwatch and asked a question: "Which part of this watch don't you think we need?"

He convinced his employees that, "When you're dealing with human parts, the best way to keep all the parts running is to treat them well."

Don't be afraid to stand up for your ideas, but don't be afraid to respect and consider the concerns of others, either.

Respect those who labor. (1 Thessalonians 5:12)

Holy Spirit, grant me both knowledge and wisdom, so that I can serve You and all Your children.

Saying the Right Thing

"May I be frank?"

If someone says that to you, the general reaction is probably one of dread. The odds are that you are not going to like what you hear. While honesty is commendable, if our truth is at someone else's expense, we need to use even higher standards.

Indian teacher and spiritual writer Eknath Eswaren has a suggestion that comes from Islamic mystics: "The Sufis advise us to speak only after our words have managed to pass through three gates. At the first gate we ask ourselves, 'Are these words true?' If so, we let them pass on; if not, back they go. At the second gate we ask, 'Are they necessary?' At the last gate we ask, 'Are they kind?'."

Truth, necessity, kindness—if we keep these things in mind, our listeners won't be sorry to let us have our say.

Never speak against the truth. (Sirach 4:25)

Spirit of Counsel, instruct me so that my words always bring help and hope to those around me.

Knocked Out by God

Most people know George Foreman as the warm, personable "grill guy" who pitches a popular kitchen appliance. But others remember the heavyweight boxing champion who has been described as surly, scary, even mean.

In 1977, George Foreman underwent a dramatic personal transformation after losing a fight he was expected to win easily. He was in the shower when he suddenly plunged into despair, thought his head and his hands were bleeding–that he had died. He began yelling, "Jesus Christ is coming alive in me."

Many have theories of what happened. Foreman says he was touched by God. Today, in addition to running his successful business and spending time with his family, Foreman regularly preaches at a small Baptist church in Houston.

We may never experience such a life-changing moment. But, if we use each day as a chance to change and grow, we will become the person God had in mind all along.

I am with you to deliver you, says the Lord. (Jeremiah 1:8)

Please touch my life and transform me, Word of the Father.

Lincoln Thinkin'

The life of one of our most admired presidents, Abraham Lincoln, holds lessons for our every day living. Historian William Lee Miller, author of *Lincoln's Virtues: An Ethical Biography*, says that some are particularly pertinent.

Don't hold a grudge. When Lincoln was denied the nomination for U.S. Senator in 1855, he told Norman Judd, who failed to support him, that he didn't hold it against him. Later, Judd nominated Lincoln for president.

Never stop learning. Lincoln held various jobs and was always reading.

Stand by your principles. When Lincoln was 10, he saw other boys torturing turtles by putting hot coals on their backs. Instead of fighting or threatening to report them, he wrote an essay focusing on the larger moral principle–that cruelty to animals is wrong–and argued the point in their one-room school.

Collaborate whenever possible. Diffuse fights with humor. Work with others rather than against them.

We can learn lessons every day, if we make the effort.

I have set you an example. (John 13:15)

Every day, Master, may all I do and say offer You praise.

Digging the Work

Why would a team of archeologists excavate the remains of an 18th-century toilet?

When Nancy Brighton and Diana Wall did just that in Manhattan, they found a wealth of information about life at the time. The hole contained coffee beans, bones, a comb, hair fasteners, buttons and the shards of 200 dishes, bowls and mugs.

It was a common practice of the time to top off a full privy with garbage in order to seal up the smell. Brighton and Wall were able to paint a fairly complete picture of daily life in the area from the refuse found in the excavation; for example, they used the collection and mixture of bones they uncovered to determine the market options of the neighborhood, dietary changes of its residents and the relative wealth of the family using the privy.

An open mind and a keen eye can reveal a world of opportunity.

Inquire first for the word of the Lord.
(1 Kings 22:5)

Lord, help us to keep an open mind and to examine all the world around us.

Teen Finds Helping Others Feels Good

When Clayton Lillard was a fifth grader he and his mother saw a girl throw out two bicycles. It seemed a good idea to retrieve and refurbish the bikes and give them to a needy family.

That was the beginning of Clayton's Backyard Crew in San Antonio. "A bike is something almost every kid wants," says Lillard. Through a program called the Angel Tree, for children with a parent in prison, he and his crew have helped make that dream come true for about 500 children.

"We...make it seem like the bike is coming from the parent who is incarcerated," he says. His mother remembers that after one youngster got a bike, he said "I knew he wouldn't forget me."

When one large family received bikes for all their kids, Clay Lillard was particular moved. "The mom was just thrilled. She was crying. It was awesome."

Indeed, good deeds are awesome.

Lay up your treasure according to the commandments of the Most High. (Sirach 29:11)

Holy Spirit, remind parents to encourage children and teenagers to think about the needs of the less fortunate.

Busy? Make a Difference Anyway

You may be busy, all day, every day. Yet there are ways you can help others if you look around for the opportunities.

Long-term unemployment is a fact of life for many. Write an encouraging note to a long out-of-work friend. Offer some practical help, from networking to a home-cooked meal.

Members of the armed services need support. Pray for them. If you know any military families, include them in an outing or ask if there's any way you can help.

Clean out closets, attic and basement for a garage sale. Donate the money to your favorite charity.

Volunteer to sort and fold clothing at a local thrift shop; or at a Meals on Wheels program or other community project.

Donate blood.

We can't do everything for everyone, but we can do something for someone–today.

Do good. (Luke 6:35)

Remind me, Jesus, of the opportunities I have to do good for others.

Me? an EMT?

"My friends think this is ridiculous. They know me to be deeply and neurotically terrified of sick people...a hypochondriac," says Jane Stern.

Even if her friends are right, she is an Emergency Medical Technician (EMT) with a volunteer fire company in a rural Connecticut town. Facing what she calls a midlife "event" not crisis, Stern realized she had to make some changes in her life. Inexplicably, she was drawn to assist the local volunteer fire company.

"It pointed me to everything cowardly I knew about myself–my fear of death and disease, my claustrophobia about being in moving vehicles that I was not driving."

Stern trained, qualified and has persevered. Author of *Ambulance Girl*, she now says "the closest I have ever felt to God has been in the back of an ambulance."

Choosing to do something hard will make us uncomfortable, but it can also make us better people.

Be brave. (Sirach 19:10)

Give me the courage, Lord, to fight my fears.

Unexpected Discovery

Professor James Murray spent decades compiling the *Oxford English Dictionary,* a massive compendium of over four hundred thousand definitions. As editor, Murray corresponded with thousands of contributors who provided definitions, quotations and other information.

One of those contributors was Dr. William Chester Minor, a former American doctor who sent submissions from his home in a small village fifty miles from Oxford, England. Murray and Minor traded correspondence for twenty years and became friends, but Minor refused Murray's every invitation to visit.

Finally, after logging ten thousand definitions from Minor, Murray decided to track down and meet his friend. It was only then that Murray discovered that Dr. Minor, a murderer, was in Broadmoor, England's harshest asylum for the criminally insane.

Even those least expected to do so can make a valuable contribution to society. Never write off a person as valueless, no matter how easy it may be to do so.

Show kindness and mercy. (Zechariah 7:9)

Lord, help us to believe in the worth of others, even when it may be hard to do so.

Get Happy!

Happy people are more reliable workers, make higher salaries, tend to get more job interviews, and have better social lives than others. They are also more likely to contribute to charity.

This data is from Dr. Ed Diener, a psychologist and specialist in happiness studies. "There are tangible benefits to happiness," he says. "Health, creativity, productivity and even altruism are all higher in happy people."

What's the secret? "There's no key to happiness," says Dr. Diener. "It's more like baking a cake. You have to have a lot of flour and eggs and sugar, and you've got to have them in the right mix.

"Certainly one of those ingredients for happiness is social relationships," he continues. "Another is temperament. And having long-term goals that are congruent with one another, and that are pleasurable to work for."

Beyond that, says Dr. Diener, the data is still developing–but let's all keep smiling in the meantime.

Happy are those who find wisdom and...get understanding. (Proverbs 3:13)

I find joy in You, Lord. May all I do always give You praise.

On Your Toes

When Arthur Mitchell walks through his Dance Theatre of Harlem, dancers stop mid-stretch and take notice. The 69-year-old legend was the first African-American male named a permanent member of a major ballet company, the New York City Ballet. But he wanted more.

After Martin Luther King, Jr.'s assassination in 1968, Mitchell founded the Dance Theatre of Harlem to help black youth by introducing them to dance. Over the years, the troupe has grown to reflect society. Dancers now come from all races and ethnicities.

"Many people, when they become successful, forget where they came from," said Mitchell. "It was very important for me to come back here. It's wonderful to feel like you're doing something that is changing people's lives."

Just think how many lives you can change by giving back, even in the smallest way. Be an active part of your community; the rewards are endless.

**A generous person will be enriched.
(Proverbs 11:25)**

Father, remind me that generosity is more than giving money. To be generous is to share with others the things that really matter to me.

An Excellent Adventure

When Tom Peters co-authored the book *In Search of Excellence*, he found he had stumbled upon a best-selling idea. Millions wanted to know the secrets behind unlocking their own potential for excellence and success.

"Excellence is difficult to define," he recently said. "It's about long-term stuff and short-term stuff. It can be a person's entire life's work or the one and only great thing a person ever did."

But Peters also underscored the fact that excellence is not always accompanied by great fanfare.

"There's the excellence of performers whose work is appreciated by millions," he explained, "but there's also the unseen excellence that occurs between friends and colleagues each day."

How will you express excellence in your life today?

Prosper the work of our hands! (Psalm 90:17)

Let us offer You thanks, God, by striving to be our best; by rising to the challenges before us, for our own good, for the good of others and for Your glory.

In Search of an Uncluttered Life

Barbara knew her home had the appearance of order and neatness, yet deep down, she also knew that this was only a façade.

"My house looks organized on the surface, but it's chaos underneath," she said, referring to the massive collection of gadgets, machines, boxes, clutter and overall "stuff" she had packed into virtually every storage space in her home.

Organization specialist Julie Morgenstern came to her rescue. She helped Barbara realize that hoarding "stuff" could be a way of fending off feelings of emptiness inside. Together, they worked on a plan to simplify Barbara's life and steer her toward counseling.

Feelings are powerful forces within humans. They seem to express themselves no matter how hard we try to quell them! Yet, once acknowledged, we can gain the ability to manage our feelings, rather than allowing feelings to manage us.

Is not life more than food, and the body more than clothing?...And can any of you by worrying add a single hour to your span of life? (Matthew 6:25,27)

Give me the courage to examine my emotions, Spirit of Counsel. Walk with me in my journey towards truth, towards You.

Road Serenity

Gridlock. Horns Blowing. Fender-benders. Road rage. These are some of the images people associate with driving to and from work. But recent studies indicate that daily commutes may not be as nerve-wracking as popularly perceived.

In fact, many people enjoy their time driving. Some have even said they'd like it to be longer because they're using the time to find solace.

In a society of hectic 24/7 schedules made possible by technology, time in a car offers a respite controlled by the driver. Some roll up the windows and blast the air conditioning, some turn up the radio and sing out loud and others find it the perfect time to pray. In any case, more and more drivers are spending that time wisely by simply changing their perspective and making it more enjoyable.

Each of us has a situation that could use a fresh outlook. What's yours?

I will hope continually, and will praise You yet more and more. (Psalm 71:14)

May I carry Your peace, Lord, wherever I may be.

Pray with Your Spouse

If you don't already join your spouse when you talk to God, consider the benefits experienced by couples who do.

In *Today's Christian Woman,* Cheri Fuller writes how she and her husband learned to pray together for specific family concerns, for example, their son's health and their finances.

"As we made our first halting efforts to pray together, we began seeing specific answers to our prayers. ...These encouraged us to keep connecting with God and with each other."

Doug and Karen, another couple she writes about, find that prayer binds them closer. Previously, notes Karen, "we'd get disconnected from each other in our different pursuits." Adds Doug, "Prayer unites our hearts into a common purpose, and we gain a deeper appreciation for what each of us does daily."

Pray with your spouse, with your family, as you express your needs and your thanks.

Pray without ceasing. (1 Thessalonians 5:17)

Pray for us and with us, Holy Spirit.

Turning Disappointment into Possibility

An honors graduate of a top-ranking university left college, filled with dreams of landing the perfect corporate job, replete with a sign-on bonus and perks anyone would envy.

Instead, much to his dismay, the only offer he received after months of job-hunting was for a position as a meter reader for a local utility company.

Although the work was arduous and hardly glamorous, the man slowly recognized the job's silver lining. The fact that it was physically demanding helped him build endurance. The tedium and repetition of the job helped him develop an ability to persevere and show up, even when he felt angry, sick or defeated. After two years, he left for a corporate job. He took with him good habits and attitudes he had nurtured in a job he had never wanted.

It takes an extraordinary person to find the positive in life's negatives. Find the extraordinary person within you.

Let us run with perseverance the race that is set before us, looking to Jesus the pioneer and perfecter of our faith. (Hebrews 12:1-2)

Christ, You showed us the way to walk through strife with dignity. Increase my faith in the value of all experiences.

Ending the Cycle of Poverty

According to Susan Hines-Brigger, writing in *St. Anthony Messenger* Magazine, one in 10 U.S. families lives in poverty. That's 33 million people.

Hines-Brigger encourages people to learn more by reading books and news articles or visiting informative websites.

Briefly living at the "poverty line" is another way. Do you know how the "poverty line" is determined? The federal government calculates the minimum amount of money needed to meet such basic needs as food, shelter, clothing, health care and transportation at $14,348, or about $275 a week for a family of three.

Hines-Brigger encourages readers to help, especially by involving the whole family. Many national and local projects such as the "Brake the Cycle of Poverty Tour," exist to raise awareness of poverty.

Everyone can do something to end poverty.

Do not rob the poor because they are poor, or crush the afflicted...for the Lord pleads their cause. (Proverbs 22:22-23)

Open my eyes to the needs of the poor, Jesus.

You Got to Do It

"You can't write no music for a fife. You can't print it. You got to do it," said Othar Turner, a musician whose first instruments were a harmonica and an empty 50-gallon lard tin.

Born to sharecroppers in Mississippi in 1908, Turner, who died at age 94, is credited with preserving a tradition of music older than the blues. The fife music he played was among the last to capture the distinctly African sounds that had been infused into the Civil War's fife and drum corps music.

Folklorists and filmmakers featured his work. Turner appeared in the jazz and heritage festivals of major urban centers around the nation, and even dropped in on *Mr. Rogers' Neighborhood*. And when he was 89 he made the first of his two full-length albums, "Everybody Hollerin' Goat."

The world would be impoverished without those who preserve the past for the future, and beauty for all.

A seal of emerald in a rich setting of gold is...music with good wine. (Sirach 32:6)

Lord, help me do and be all that You have put in my heart and leave the rest to You.

Success with Jelly

In 1859, Robert Augustus Chesebrough had reason to be down. At 22, he had already failed at selling kerosene and getting into the oil business.

Unemployed, he started hanging out with oil rig operators. They told him about an oil by-product called rod wax that seemed to have healing powers. Chesebrough carried a bucket of the sludge home. He then spent the next few years acting as his own guinea pig, cutting and burning his arms and hands, applying the wax's essential ingredient–a colorless, odorless jelly–to his wounds. They healed.

So, the world got "Vaseline" from the German word for water and a Greek word for olive oil. By 1874, he was selling a jar a minute, with people rubbing the salve not only on scrapes, cuts and chapped lips, but also on wooden furniture and cracked leather. This was the foundation of the Chesebrough-Ponds empire.

No one is guaranteed success, but persistence makes it possible.

Human success is in the hand of the Lord. (Sirach 10:5)

Hear me when I call in the darkness, Father; send me Your strength and Your light.

Investing to Make a Difference

We are often told that money is the root of all evil. Actually, in his epistle to Timothy, Paul warns that the *love* of money is the problem. Money itself can be good, necessary. In a feature about money, *Utne* magazine concluded that "you don't need to be a big-bucks investor or philanthropist to make a difference."

Hazel Henderson, an economist suggests investing in funds that are "socially responsible."

Marjorie Kelly, editor of *Business Ethics* suggests investing in local institutions that make loans for inner-city development, low-income housing or small-business help.

Jacob Needleman, a philosophy professor, suggests using money "to further one's own pursuit of truth and inner development." The world, he says, needs "men and women of wisdom and conscience" who "understand the Good."

You work hard for every dollar you have. Pray and study to use those dollars wisely for your own good and the good of all.

The love of money is a root of...evil, and in their eagerness to be rich some have wandered away from the faith. (1 Timothy 6:10)

Inspire corporate and personal financial decisions, Holy Spirit.

Carving Our Lives

Sculptor Sergio Dolfi has worked with wood for more than 60 years. When he sees a piece of teak, ebony, or walnut, he looks for inspiration in an abstract twist or interesting flow of grain. Occasionally he enhances his work with semi-precious stones, ivory, or coral.

Dolfi can't always see the end before he begins working. "Sometimes I know what it's going to be," he claims. "Other times I start to carve and later discover what I'll do."

Most of us could say the same. When our hearts draw us to new adventures, new friends, or perhaps a new job, we can't tell how it will turn out. But like Dolfi, we can move forward, eager to discover what treasures may unfold.

Says the artist: "It is a very satisfying feeling when a piece turns out the way I want it to be."

Steadfast love surrounds those who trust in the Lord. (Psalm 32:10)

Make me brave enough to trust You, God.

Mustached Marvels

Some people run to raise money; some walk; others grow mustaches.

That's what a group of New York City businessmen are doing for the Make-A-Wish foundation, a nonprofit organization that aims to grant the wishes of children facing terminal or life-threatening illnesses.

The mustache growing pledge rally is officially known as Mustaches for Kids. The goal of these normally mustache-less men is to raise $6000, the average amount it takes to grant one child's wish.

The process is simple: grow as full a mustache as possible within six-weeks and have friends and relatives sponsor the effort. Mustache Checkpoint pictures are then posted once a week so everyone can monitor the action. The rules are no beards, goatees, or anything that could be considered a joke.

As the organizers say, "The Mustache is more in the heart than on the face."

We can all find ways to do good while having a good time.

Even the hairs of your head are counted. (Matthew 10:30)

Jesus, grant me a creative spirit that I may better imitate You.

The Color of Love

The late Barbara Vernon Bailey, also known as Sister Mary Barbara, grew up in a wealthy home in Shropshire, England. Despite her privileged life, by her early twenties she had chosen to live as a cloistered Augustinian nun.

Knowing that his daughter had a propensity for drawing, Bailey's father, Cuthbert Bailey, an executive at Doulton, makers of fine china, brought her paints and paper. Soon the company was using her whimsical drawings of a close-knit family of rabbits engaged in everyday activities on children's china.

But between her superior's lack of encouragement and lack of time after she had fulfilled her monastic duties, Barbara Vernon Bailey stopped drawing. That means that today the rare surviving cups and bowls featuring Bailey's "Bunnykin" designs fetch thousands of dollars at auctions and sales.

Thank God for the artist in yourself; the artists you know.

We have gifts that differ according to the grace given. (Romans 12:6)

Help us nurture our gifts, Lord, remembering always that they come from You.

All News Is Good News

Joseph Zisa thinks that most daily newspapers "do a pretty good job of highlighting the negative," so he decided to emphasize the positive.

With the help of his wife and daughter, Zisa launched a free newspaper called *The County Seat* in Hackensack, New Jersey, to highlight the good happenings within the community. "At long last, the achievements of our populace will be brought to light and spotlighted," says Zisa, "Everything is local. ...Everything is positive."

The search for the positive will always prove more rewarding than settling for the negative.

Jealousy and anger shorten life, and anxiety brings on premature old age. (Sirach 30:24)

Help me emphasize the positives in my life, Lord. Help me to always seek what is good, true and beautiful.

Operation Haiti

It all started with a walk.

The parishioners of St. Boniface in Quincy, Massachusetts wanted to use half the money they made from a walk for hunger to support the poorest of the poor in Haiti. Unable to find an agency to take the money, several parishioners traveled to Haiti to deliver the funds themselves.

What they found was a town of 40,000 people called Fond-des-Blancs in desperate need of medical facilities. What they also found was a new purpose for their own lives. Parishioners returned to Boston and created the St. Boniface Haiti Foundation to raise money to build a small clinic in Fond-des-Blancs.

Today, some parishioners travel to Haiti several times a year, bringing supplies to what has grown into a 20-bed hospital complete with an operating room and a staff of 50 including three Haitian doctors.

It's amazing what we can do—one step at a time.

Help the poor for the Commandment's sake. (Sirach 29:9)

Loving God, energize me to create hope out of despair.

More than Just a Scientific Mind

The name Albert Einstein probably brings several things to mind: science, the theory of relativity, the Nobel Prize, frizzy hair, brilliance. However, Einstein also made several contributions to international peace.

Einstein had very strong anti-war feelings throughout his life and was an avid supporter of civil rights. In 1939, he warned the White House that Nazi Germany was developing atomic weapons. In 1944, to contribute to the war effort against the Nazis, he hand wrote his 1905 paper on special relativity to be sold at auction. It raised $6 million dollars.

"Nothing that I can do will change the structure of the universe," Einstein said, "but maybe, by raising my voice, I can help in the greatest of all causes—goodwill among men and peace on earth."

Raise your voice for a good cause.

Blessed are the peacemakers for they will be called children of God. (Matthew 5:9)

Grant me the strength to stand up for something I believe in, Prince of Peace.

Making the Years Count

Marguerite Kueckelhan of Washington state holds a shotput record and has played exhibition basketball against the Seattle Supersonics. Pretty remarkable for a centenarian.

Today, some 40,000 persons in the United States have hit the century mark; by the year 2050, that number is expected to be one million.

"The secret to becoming a centenarian is a combination of genetics, lifestyle choices, mental acuity and just plain luck," notes Dr. Thomas T. Perls, author and associate professor of medicine at Boston University School of Medicine.

Kueckelhan, a widow, lives alone in an independent living facility. She eats lightly, principally vegetables and fruits. "Death is coming," she says, matter-of-factly. "I accept it as part of life, but I don't think about it."

She lives each day to the fullest. "Being 90 or 100 is no excuse for inactivity," she says. "I think it's the spirit within you."

A spirit, it seems, that is ageless.

Wisdom is a fountain of life. (Proverbs 16:22)

From my first breath to my last, I celebrate Your love for me, Lord.

A Legacy of Kindness

The Potato Famine of 1848 forced many families, including James and Maggie Fitzpatrick, to flee Ireland.

Destitute, the Fitzpatricks and their infant daughter Phoebe left for Canada on a "coffin ship," so named because 20 to 40 percent of passengers perished on the voyage. James and Maggie died, leaving Phoebe an orphan.

A young sailor was ordered to throw Phoebe overboard along with the bodies, as there was no one onboard who would look after the infant and no family awaiting her in Canada.

Instead, the young sailor cared for Phoebe for the remainder of the journey and then placed her with a kind French-Canadian family.

Phoebe grew up strong, married and had a family of her own. And though his name is not remembered, the goodness of that young sailor lives on through each generation of Phoebe's descendents.

Life is God's free and precious gift. Cherish it. Nurture it.

Choose life...loving the Lord your God, obeying Him, and holding fast to Him.
(Deuteronomy 30:19, 20)

Holy Trinity, help us appreciate Your gift of life.

Simmons' Secret

Ruth Simmons grew up as the twelfth child of sharecroppers in East Texas. When she reached school age her dad took a job in a factory while her mother found work as a maid.

Her humble circumstances did not stand in the way of a great education. Eventually she earned a doctorate in Romance languages and literatures from Harvard University.

Named president of Brown University in the fall of 2000, Simmons was asked to speak about leadership.

"I try to anticipate the ways I can improve what I do and not allow my personal weaknesses to get in the way of doing my job," she said. "I try to recognize as quickly as I can when I'm making mistakes or when I'm on the wrong path. The sooner you can acknowledge your mistakes–but not punish yourself for them–the better a leader you are."

Don't be afraid to lead. Just know where you are going.

The rule of the intelligent person is well ordered. (Sirach 10:1)

Holy Spirit, shower us with Your gifts of fortitude, knowledge and wisdom.

Slow Down

California's Mission San Juan Capistrano, more than 200 years old, is famous for being the place where swallows return every year on or about March 19th, the feast of St. Joseph.

Now it is undergoing much-needed and painstaking work to halt the crumbling of the Great Stone Church and conserve seven adobe buildings. The administrator of the nonprofit historic Mission says that in this restoration work "there is no such thing as a shortcut." If workers aren't careful, even more of the walls plastered with mortar will crumble and turn to dust.

Graduate students studying historic preservation also work on the mission site getting hands-on experience repairing, restoring and reinforcing church walls. Progress is necessarily slow and they "measure their progress in inches per week."

Although you wouldn't know it by the pace of contemporary life, faster isn't always better. Some things need time.

Every matter has its time and way. (Ecclesiastes 8:6)

May we learn to appreciate and savor the moment, Jesus.

What a Smile Can Lead To

"I've noticed you each Sunday, and you smile a lot. My grandma died four years ago, and I miss her. Will you be my 'Church Grandma'? Love, Brianna."

These words were written to Minnesotan Lorraine Halli by a fellow churchgoer, 12-year-old Brianna Hagen. After speaking with Brianna's mother, Lorraine wrote back, "Of course, I'll be your Church Grandma!"

The match was made in heaven. Halli was a widow whose three children and seven grand-children lived out of state. She has since become a part of the Hagen family, sharing every special occasion and many of the in-between moments.

Halli writes, "There really are no accidents. Somehow, Brianna had known just who to chose as her Church Grandma—a choice that filled a place in my heart I hadn't even known was empty."

See what a smile can lead to? Try yours.

The wise smile quietly. (Sirach 21:20)

May they see Your face when I smile, Jesus.

A Chocolate Egg, A Smuggler's Dream

It's hard to believe, but one of the hottest contraband items of the season is not some rare jewel or trendy designer purse. It's a foil-wrapped hollow chocolate egg containing tiny toys.

Legal in 100 countries but banned in the U.S., it is fast becoming a coveted confection. Some people are buying hundreds of the surprise eggs and handing them out at family gatherings, office parties, or to clients.

So why are they banned here? The U.S. Consumer Product Safety Commission says they are a choking hazard because a thumb-sized plastic capsule with a little toy inside is hidden within the candy. This creates a danger for children.

No one wants excessive rules and regulations. But, respect for laws and protecting children are hallmarks of good citizenship.

Seek justice. (Isaiah 1:17)

Instill a respect for the rule of law in us Lord, so that our nation may grow into a nation of, by and for all the people.

A Fisher of Souls

To Sister of Mercy Carol Anne Corley, fly-fishing is serious spiritual business.

She and a partner formed the U.S. Youth Fly-Fishing Association in 1999 to interest young people in the sport and train them in its techniques. They often work with youngsters from broken homes or with other problems. "You thank God for the kids you get and you pray for the ones you don't," says Sister Carol Anne Corley.

She also believes fly-fishing offers more than coordination and relaxation. She believes it has a spiritual power that rivals prayer. She says the countless hours she has stood waist-deep in rivers watching trout rise to her flies have enriched her soul. "At times...it is prayer...a way of praising God."

One can pray any where, any time, about any thing. Take every opportunity to talk with God.

Devote yourself to prayer. (Colossians 4:2)

Abba, remind me that prayer is mindfulness and communication with You.

Getting the Best of Grief

Maggie found herself perpetually sad after her mother's death. She waited for the emptiness to leave her, but it just wouldn't.

Her four-year-old daughter, finding her on the couch, crying silently, looked in her face and said: "Mommy, I love you, you know. So why are you always so sad?"

In that moment, Maggie realized that her love for her mother would always be with her. But her child and her husband were here today, filled with great love for her too.

Nothing is the same after the death of someone we love. Grief is terrible. But the time comes when moving on is necessary if we are to live healthy and, yes, happy lives. The challenge is to transform a grieving heart into an open heart.

Sometimes it just takes the wisdom of a child–found in an open smiling face and to-the-heart words–to make that happen.

Be comforted for your grief. For...a sorrowful heart saps one's strength. (Sirach 38:17,18)

Embrace my sadness, Divine Master, so that I may find strength in Your love.

Getting Even? Heaven Help Us!

Treated unfairly? Deliberately hurt by maliciousness? Misunderstood, gossiped about, discriminated against?

Get even—in a manner of speaking! Here's what Jessie Rice Sandberg, author of *Letting People Off the Hook,* advises:

- Keep a list on the refrigerator, on the bathroom mirror, in a convenient place on your desk (unless people at the office are on the list) of those who have hurt you, of difficult situations.
- Every day pray for these people; about these situations.

Praying for people will enable you to better understand them and their problems. Praying will also relieve your stress.

And finally, prayer will enable you to represent God's faithful merciful love to the unlovable and difficult.

Love your enemies and pray for those who persecute you. (Matthew 5:44)

Dear Father, help me to pray for my enemies.

Walking in Confidence

Ruth VanReken always wanted to be a nurse. She became one. Then, through a series of events, she began to focus on helping internationally mobile families deal with issues they face while raising children cross-culturally.

"I couldn't have prepared for this because I didn't even know it was a topic," she says, marveling at the path that led to her work. From her perspective today, VanReken easily recognizes the hand of God in her life. She grew up as a missionary kid, became a missionary, and raised her own children abroad.

VanReken's journey has given her the confidence to walk with others through their difficulties. "I know God's at work even when I have no idea how a particular situation may turn out," she says. "God prepared me perfectly for this one tiny niche in His kingdom."

We can't always understand what God does. We can always trust Him. That's why it's called faith.

Trust in the Lord with all your heart and do not rely on your own insight. In all your ways acknowledge Him, and He will make straight your paths. (Proverbs 3:5-6)

Spirit of God, increase our faith, our hope, our love in You!

A Bitter Pill to Swallow: Anger

For many of us, anger is perhaps one of the most difficult emotions to cope with. It is hard to confront and sometimes, even harder to let go of.

The Huichol Indians of Mexico seem to have found a unique and effective way to cleanse the soul of anger. Several times a year, the villagers gather around a great fire for a group confession, where each individual admits to any wrongdoings. Afterward, the injured parties confront the wrong-doer.

Harsh words and tears follow. Yet, there are no rights or wrongs, only resolutions. As the sun rises, all is forgiven and the incident is left behind. A massive celebration concludes the ceremony.

Repressing anger is not only unproductive, it is unhealthy. Sometimes, the best way to get to the end of a problem is to go through it.

Do not let the sun go down on your anger. (Ephesians 4:26)

God, strengthen me in my dealings with others. Give me the courage to confront my own feelings.

The "Sermon on the Mount" Updated

An article in *Utne* magazine offers a delightfully plain version of Jesus' "Sermon on the Mount," (Matthew 5-7). Here are some of its points:

- Those who live gently will know gentleness.
- The generous will be rich.
- Speak simply.
- Love those who curse you…use you…persecute you.
- Let good acts be done without fanfare.
- (Pray) in the privacy of your own heart.
- Conduct yourself with dignity.
- Look with a clear eye upon all.
- Pay no attention to your neighbor's little offenses. Examine your own actions.
- Don't be wasteful.

God, your neighbors, all Creation, indeed you yourself, need you to be the "salt of the earth" and "the light of the world." Begin today.

Do justice…love kindness, walk humbly with your God(.) (Micah 6:8)

Holy Spirit, encourage me.

Angels of Love

Caring Collection, Inc., is a thriving nonprofit organization whose volunteers' creations have raised thousands of dollars for cancer research.

It started small. In 1982 Bobbie Burnett wanted to cheer up her friend, Susie, who was being treated for leukemia. Susie had three young children, an unemployed husband and no health insurance. So she used her artistic talents to create a three-dimensional stained glass angel for Susie. Susie loved it and displayed it in her hospital room. Soon others wanted an angel too.

The former art instructor taught friends how to make angels in various sizes and sold them to help pay Susie's medical expenses. Sadly, Susie died – but the angel project continued.

"I had planned on making only one angel as a gift to Susie," says Ms. Burnett. "But that one angel completely directed my life."

You never know when a gift you give may make a difference in your own life. Be generous.

He will command His angels concerning you to guard you in all your ways. (Psalm 91:11)

Inspire us to find creative ways to share Your love, Jesus.

Selling Futures

In her job as director of communications for a film distributor, Kris Percival saw one movie after another, some top notch and others that were dreadful. Percival had to sell the flick no matter what.

This whole less-than-truthful angle in her career took its toll. Percival started to think about her second career choice—teaching. Earlier, she'd convinced herself that teaching wasn't "powerful, prestigious or lucrative enough."

But after six years in the publicity business, Percival decided to do something "that's actually helping people," she said. She went back to school for a master's degree in education, and gave her film job notice. She even held a stoop sale and sold her cell phone.

Today she uses the skills she honed as a publicist to convince a roomful of children that math is fun. And she loves it.

It's never too late to make a change, to make a difference.

Do not forsake My teaching. (Proverbs 3:1)

Grant me the gift of Your wisdom, Lord, that I may know how best to serve You.

Taking on the Crown

Viggo Mortensen just didn't know if he wanted the part. The actor originally hired to play the character had been fired. The project was already two months into preproduction and he'd have to fly to New Zealand the next day if he accepted. Moreover, he was unfamiliar with the project's source material. Mortensen turned to his son for advice.

"What character?" his son asked. The actor checked his notes. "Strider?" "That's great," his son replied. "He's cool."

Mortensen accepted the part based on his son's enthusiasm, and went on to play Aragorn, the human king hiding as a ranger known as Strider, in Peter Jackson's film adaptation of J.R.R. Tolkien's trilogy *The Lord of the Rings*. The acclaimed movies were nominated for dozens of Oscars and grossed several billion dollars worldwide.

Trust in chance and in those you love. It could bring unexpected rewards.

In God I trust. (Psalm 56:4)

Help us to appreciate those we love always, Blessed Lord.

To Feed the Hungry

One day while sitting in suburban comfort, the reality of hunger hit Pam Koner. Her newspaper showed a girl lying on a bare, dirty mattress eating her one meal of the day—some pasta with neck bones.

"I got up and…walked into the living room and said, 'I've got to do something,'" recalls Ms. Koner. She started Family-to-Family which has become a community effort.

Families in Hastings, New York, now adopt needy families in Pembroke, Illinois, one of America's poorest communities. They send monthly food boxes that might include extras like shampoo, diapers and instant coffee.

An overnight shipping company offers free deliveries, another company donates boxes and a supermarket contributes gift certificates. Elderly neighbors who can't shop send donations.

In return, recipients write to donors. One mother of six children appreciates the end-of-the-month box which arrives when food stamps and food run low. "It's truly a blessing."

Open your eyes, your heart and your hand to others.

Share your bread with the hungry. (Isaiah 58:7)

May we feed those hungry in soul and body, Jesus.

Learning to Play

Mary Mohler, who has five children, believes kids learn a great deal from play. Among her suggestions for parents:

- Get down on the floor and once you're down there, let the children be in charge of the game.
- Learn how to roughhouse, albeit gently. Your surprised youngsters will be consumed with contagious giggles.
- Find it hard to get into your children's games? Set a timer if you have to, but then throw yourself wholeheartedly into whatever captures your children's imaginations for the entire time you are playing.

Open yourself to the gifts and lessons the children in your life have to share with you. It's an easy way to experience how richly generosity is rewarded.

Live as children of light. (Ephesians 5:8)

Remind us, Creator, how important it is to nourish the little ones in our lives. Show us how to play, laugh and love together.

Winning *Really* Isn't Everything

The 1996 U.S. Amateur Golf Championship proved to be one of the most exciting and dramatic sports events of that year. The finals featured Steve Scott and Tiger Woods and was marked by an extremely close race up to the very end.

What most people don't know is that the very end of the match was largely driven by an act of extraordinary integrity by Scott. As Woods carefully approached his next putt, Scott reminded his opponent to move his ball back to its original spot before putting. Had Woods not done so, he would have been penalized two strokes and lost the championship. Woods made the correction, and sank the putt, winning the match in sudden death.

Steve Scott valued his integrity more than winning the match. How much would you forfeit to preserve your character?

Love truth and peace. (Zechariah 8:19)

It isn't always easy to be a person of integrity when winning and "being the best" are over-valued, Jesus. Help me focus on Your values of truth and integrity.

Unlikely Beginnings

Carol David's past bears little resemblance to her present. Director of an emergency care facility for homeless families, she is organized, decisive and businesslike under pressure.

David originally wanted to pursue a life in the arts. Growing up in the Bronx, New York, neighborhood in which she now works, she envisioned being an illustrator–and wrote a children's book in the hopes of being a published author someday.

What drew her to a life of service to the needy? "I had a strong family," she says. "I knew a lot of people who didn't. Even if you're in a crisis, even if family things break down, you can still bring the family up again."

A strong sense of family can provide the strength for a lifetime of positive choices. Take time to solidify your own family's ties.

Things that the Lord hates...one who sows discord in a family. (Proverbs 6:16,19)

God, we are all part of Your human family, each of us precious in Your sight. Knowing this reminds me of my individual worth and value.

A Sparkle of Light

A brewery exploded in Dublin, Ireland, destroying a 130-year-old stained glass window in a neighboring church and scattering the pieces like a jigsaw puzzle. The seemingly insurmountable task of putting those pieces back together fell to the Abbey Stained Glass Studio.

The window was restored to the church a year later. "One could almost hear the gasps as the glass sparkled like it must have when it was originally installed," said Managing Director Ken Ryan.

Ryan and his workforce are dedicated to restoring old and damaged ecclesiastical stained glass paintings of renowned artists. "We are most fortunate to house a wealth of stained glass by artists of the highest caliber," Ryan said. Without these studio artists, many masterful paintings of light would have been destroyed and forgotten.

Let us not forget the masterpieces of our own time while preserving those of the past for future generations.

Every artisan and master artisan who labors by night as well as by day...is diligent...careful to finish their work. (Sirach 38:27)

Holy Spirit, inspire and encourage artists and crafts persons to illuminate the world with Your light.

Reaching Young Lawbreakers

Upset with a system that imprisons young offenders, many of them drug addicted, but doesn't prepare them for release, Judy Garvey decided she had to get involved if things were to improve.

After researching to see what programs had worked elsewhere, Garvey assembled a group of like-minded citizens and started Volunteers for Hancock County (Maine) Jail Residents.

In cooperation with law enforcement authorities, volunteers bring concerts, classes and companionship to the prisoners.

And now when a young inmate is released, he or she gets a free hot breakfast and a "release packet" with a meal coupon, a phone card, and a list of free community services.

The group's goal is to build a bridge between the young ex-offenders and the community; to be mentors; and, hopefully, to reduce recidivism and keep the neighborhood safe.

Incarcerated people were once "the neighbor next door" and most will be that again.

**I was in prison and you visited me.
(Matthew 25:36)**

Enable us to persevere, Lord, as we guide and support troubled young people.

Rocker Gets Good Advice

Some advice is worth taking.

Carlos Santana always loved music. He even played guitar as a little boy on the streets of his native Mexico. When he and his family later moved to the United States, he had little interest in his high school classes and it showed. He failed everything except art. That's when his art teacher told young Carlos, "There's no room for anyone giving 50 percent. You should do 150 percent. Whatever you're doing, or whatever you're trying to be. Whether you're a painter or a musician or a fireman."

Carlos Santana went on to record dozens of albums and to be inducted into the Rock and Roll Hall of Fame. But it all happened because he heeded the advice to "do 150 percent."

So, before you ignore advice, at least think about it. Then use your good judgment to decide your own future.

Listen to advice and accept instruction, that you may gain wisdom for the future. (Proverbs 19:20)

Spirit of Wisdom, help me hear You when You speak through others—and to know when You don't.

She's His Oldest Friend

Late in the afternoon, she knew to look for him. It was their time together–one hour a day, three times a week. They read her mail; she pressed him about whether he was exercising.

An ordinary meeting between friends? Yes. Except Elvis Checo, 20, is a volunteer and Margaret Oliver, 93, is a nursing home resident. But 73 years of separation collapses when they are together. "It's like we're the same age," says Oliver.

Bringing together old and young can ease the loneliness many older people experience. And the young can profit from the accumulated wisdom of the elderly. After all, they've seen a thing or two.

"Reaching old age, you don't feel you're a part of the world," says Checo. "My goal is to make her still feel part of it."

An amazing journey takes place in that one hour–love bridges the generations.

Rise before the aged. (Leviticus 19:32)

Your love, Father, is ageless; Your kindness is to all generations.

A Model for Healing

The United States exports rice, automobiles, computers and recently, medical care to Ghana.

Dr. Kathryn Challoner, an associate professor of clinical emergency medicine at the University of Southern California at Los Angeles, was one of ten doctors who traveled to Ghana at their own expense for a symposium on emergency medical care.

They lectured and conducted workshops together with the staff of the medical college at the University of Uhana in Accra, Ghana's capital. The aim was to help local doctors design their own emergency system.

Dr. Challoner found that both sides taught lessons. Ghana is an active member of the United Nations. And the current Secretary-General, Kofi Annan, calls Ghana home. "This country has resolutely remained at peace," she says. "It's a model to West Africa–and maybe to all of us."

Build peace in your life and share it.

Render...judgments that... make for peace, do not devise evil against one another, and love no false oath...love...peace. (Zechariah 8:16-17,19)

Prince of Peace, whisper peace to us that we may whisper it to a world desperate for peace.

Volunteering their Love

Volunteers at animal shelters all over the country care for the animals housed there. While some volunteers care for any animal, some prefer to concentrate on those that are passed over time and time again.

"Prospective owners don't want the dog with bald spots, or the cat with a missing eye," says Matt Marino, a volunteer at a New York shelter. "These animals need extra attention, but instead they are starved for the love their eyes beg for."

While the animals wait for a caring owner to come along, the volunteers act as foster owners, walking and brushing the animals, and giving them crucial human contact.

"It's rewarding to see how much ten minutes outside a cage can improve an animal's demeanor," Marino adds. "Then, fortunately, they're more likely to get adopted."

Seek out God's creatures that are most in need of your affection and care.

God made the wild animals of the earth. (Genesis 1:25)

Lord, watch over neglected creatures everywhere.

Working Toward Goals

If there is an important goal you're determined to achieve, you probably already realize that you won't necessarily get there either quickly or easily.

In fact, some people spend an entire lifetime in pursuit of their passion or for a great cause. It often entails hard work, patience, and yet more hard work.

Many of those who worked on the New York City subway system ("born" in 1904) never lived to see the fruits of their labor. Many were killed in construction accidents.

"If events from a century ago show anything clearly, it is that our urban forebears suffered greatly for the sake of the mass transit we have inherited," according to one recent newspaper account.

The present is built on the lives and labors of the past. If you would understand today, learn about yesterday.

Let us now sing the praises...of our ancestors. ...whose righteous deeds have not been forgotten. (Sirach 44:1,10)

Guide me toward a greater understanding of Your ways, Lord. Help me to persevere with patience.

Inspiration in Life, Death

Gifted tennis player and student Mike MacKinnon was a Hawaii state finalist when he was tragically killed in a car crash. But his ability to inspire didn't end.

His teammates believed that what made Mike so special was that he "embodied the team's ideals...compassion, humility and an unending desire for excellence."

In this way, even after death, Mike's influence pervades the team, just as he inspired teammates in life. For example, team captain Richard Salem volunteers at a local Head Start program.

Every choice, every action can empower and inspire others or it can discourage them. Since, as John Donne wrote, "no man is an island" our actions are important. We touch others more than we know, sometimes even more than they know.

Assist your neighbor to the best of your ability. (Sirach 29:20)

Spirit of Wisdom, make us courageous.

American Ginseng: Useful or Not?

The mystique and high demand for an herb called ginseng was as strong in 1787 as it has been recently.

Daniel Boone sent a barge load of dried ginseng to market in Philadelphia from his trading post in what is now West Virginia.

In 1859 there was a "ginseng rush." Rumors of the plant's near-magical properties fueled steady demand.

In recent times, however, some case studies have shown that ginseng has little more effect on stamina and energy than placebos. Other studies suggest that ginseng may have antioxidant properties as well as the ability to help lower blood sugar. Still other studies have shown that Asian and American ginseng have different properties. Still, the demand for ginseng remains robust.

How do we determine what's healthful? Popular opinion? Fads and crazes? Scientific research? As in so many areas, we need to obtain reliable information and exercise good judgment.

Take care of your health. (Sirach 18:19)

Give me the strength to stand alone, Lord, rather than just follow the crowd.

A Great Big Tale

One night a little French boy named Mathieu didn't feel well. To distract him, his mother, Cecile, regaled him and his brother Laurent with the story of an orphaned elephant who went to Paris and got himself into trouble. Fortunately the elephant's cousins came and persuaded him to return to his jungle home.

The next morning, the boys repeated the wonderful tale for their father. Jean de Brunhoff wrote the story down and illustrated it for his sons. Thus, Babar the elephant was born.

Brunhoff wrote and illustrated another seven Babar books before his death in 1937; Laurent continued the work, adding another 40 titles to the series.

And so it was that a loving mother, generously responding to the need of her child, brought joy to youngsters around the world for generations.

Joy is a sign of God's presence. Bring joy to children.

Let the little children come to Me. (Matthew 19:14)

Remind me, Loving Father, that You are with me in things both great and small.

Champion of Change on Madison Avenue

The fact that she was one of the first women to own a national advertising agency is impressive enough. But that Franchellie Margaret Cadwell worked to improve the way women and the elderly were depicted in advertising illustrates the true visionary spirit "Frankie" Cadwell possessed.

In 1970 Cadwell realized that "advertising makes women look as if they have the mentality of a six-year old." She worked to change that perception, and tirelessly polled women and the elderly on their opinions and concerns about advertising in hopes of making a change.

What's more, she encouraged consumers to fight back by not buying products and services that used degrading or insulting methods to promote their products.

Voice your concerns to companies and manufacturers if you don't like their advertising methods. As a consumer, you possess influence. Use it!

When justice is done, it is a joy to the righteous. (Proverbs 21:15)

Jesus, give me a genuine sense of my innate dignity as a person.

Why Jury Duty Matters

The U.S. Constitution guarantees defendants in criminal cases and litigants in civil cases the right to trial by jury. Yet jury service doubtless intrudes on jurors' everyday lives.

Lois Burch O'Brian, writing in *The Buffalo News* about her experience, said: "Jury duty is a great thing, although not at first, when you realize...all of the inconveniences you will suffer to spend your days in court...However, when you and your fellow jurors walk out of that jury room with a verdict, you will know it was worth it."

She found that during deliberations, "I persuaded and was persuaded, I learned and hope I taught. If you were to ask my fellow jurors their impressions...I'm sure you'd get eleven different opinions. But those different views resulted in one verdict. And that's a good thing."

Jury duty is critically important. When you're called, serve.

The Lord grant you wisdom...to judge His people with justice. (Sirach 45:26)

Holy Spirit, grant me Your good counsel when it is truly necessary that I judge others.

Sowing Seeds of Renewal

Veterinarian John Anderson and his wife bought a 50-acre farm in California in the early 1970s. While he didn't know much about grasslands, he did know that the near-complete absence of wildlife in his fields was a sign of something perilous.

After research, he learned that years of monoculture (single crop) farming had made the land barren, unable to sustain the quail, fox and deer that had once flourished there.

Anderson embarked on a successful effort to restore the native grasslands and hence the wildlife. His farm now teems with wildlife.

The natural world is an amazingly diverse and fruitful place. Human beings eliminate that variety at their own peril and the Earth's. What can you do to conserve the health of the Earth, our home?

The Lord...formed the earth and made it...He did not create it a chaos, he formed it to be inhabited! (Isaiah 45:18)

Lord, instincts are Your gift for my self-preservation. Thank You for guiding me through life.

Testing Her Perseverance

For most seventh-graders, the prospect of taking the required year-end competency exam is not appealing. But Sarah Ferreira fought for the opportunity to endure the exam.

Because Ferreira has cystic fibrosis, a disease of the respiratory and digestive systems, Massachusetts officials agreed that she could be exempted from it. Officials thought the test would be too stressful.

But Ferreira says, "I really had to take it. I like school. I just like keeping up with my work." Her determination convinced teachers that she was strong enough to withstand the hours of questions and essays, and she successfully completed the exam.

Some people refuse to let life's obstacles and setbacks, even serious illness, derail them. Others focus on every little thing that goes wrong. Whom do you aspire to be?

A tree, if it is cut down...will sprout again... Though its root grows old...and its stump dies... yet at the scent of water it will bud and put forth branches like a young plant. (Job 14:7,8,9)

Lord God, please help me see the possibilities in all situations.

Connect or Divide

Television producer Joss Whedon remembers a speech given to the staff when he worked as a writer on a sitcom with a famous and controversial star. That comic, a frequent topic in the tabloid headlines of the time, denigrated the writers and threatened to fire them all if any ever spoke to the press. The vulgar and insulting episode left Whedon with a bitter taste in his mouth.

"It made me realize, at that moment," said Whedon, "that every time somebody opens their mouth they have an opportunity to do one of two things—connect or divide... I'm shocked that there are so many people who live to divide."

"Connecting is the most important thing," he stresses, "and actually an easy thing to do."

Start small—with a word of thanks to a co-worker, family member or even the morning coffee person—and build from there. Respect can foster strong bonds and surprising fruits.

A word fitly spoken is like apples of gold in a setting of silver. (Proverbs 25:11)

Holy God, help us to seek connection rather than division.

New Directions

Scientists tell us that the continents of South America and Africa became separated from each other about 90 million years ago. South America began moving west, eventually crashing into an oceanic plate moving in the opposite direction. One result was the formation of the Andes Mountains.

Today this world-famous mountain range features spectacular volcanic cones, snow-capped peaks, and lush valleys. It is home to national parks and exotic birds. And it all began with wrenching separation.

How often we resist separation in our lives. We cling to familiar jobs, cities and routines. Many find satisfaction in routine. But those who seek significant, positive change may do well to consider the development of the earth. Yes, the process included cataclysmic events. But what loveliness resulted!

**What goodness and beauty are His!
(Zechariah 9:17)**

Lord, help me see each reflection of Your beauty.

On Baseball and Life

By the mid-1800s, baseball was becoming *the* sport to play in America. Walt Whitman was a great proponent of the pastime, but not because he admired a good sliding curve ball. He argued that time spent outside would produce a better class of men, and that was good for America.

Whitman wrote in the *Brooklyn Eagle:* "Let us enjoy life a little. Let us go forth a while and get better air in our lungs. Let us leave our close rooms and the dust and corruption of stagnant places, and taste some of the good things Providence has scattered around us so liberally."

Too often we get caught up in our work or watching television and pass on opportunities to grab some fresh air. Whether a row on a lake, a twilight stroll or a game of baseball, take time to "enjoy life a little." You'll be the better for it.

Which of you...covets many days to enjoy good? Keep your tongue from...deceit. Depart from evil, and do good; seek peace, and pursue it. (Psalm 34:12-14)

Father, You have bestowed upon us a world full of wonders; let us enjoy it and be thankful.

United We Stand

California redwoods are amazing for a number of reasons. Some reach 300 feet in height and are more than 2,500 years old. People stand in awe of them.

But these huge trees, the tallest on earth, have a surprisingly shallow root system. For this reason, it seems logical to think that they are potentially quite vulnerable. And yet, when storms batter them, they remain standing. What accounts for this?

Writer Robert J. Morgan explains that the reason redwood trees don't topple in gusting winds is their roots all intertwine. They're locked together.

"When the storms come or the winds blow, the redwoods stand...and they don't stand alone, for all the trees support and protect each other."

The same holds for us. A good support system can be a bulwark against the routine stresses of everyday life as well as life's major storms. People are amazing, too.

Human beings...You have made them a little lower than God, and crowned them with glory and honor. (Psalm 8:4,5)

Creator, instill in us a great appreciation for the wonders of Your world.

Writing Prayers

After a long, frustrating morning which included scolding her son for breaking his lunch box, Jan Johnson retreated to her bed, but not to sleep. Instead, she pulled out a spiral notebook and began to spread her grief and frustration before God.

Johnson created her spiritual diary to help her overcome and perhaps understand everyday challenges. "In that quiet space, we develop a conversation with God, offering our self-absorbed ideas and then allowing them to become swallowed up in the goals God is cultivating for us," she explains.

Some who keep spiritual journals write every day; others like Johnson, do it when they feel the need. For her, the written reflections, especially when reread, help answer one important question, "What is God doing with my life?"

So the next time life hits you hard, or you don't know what to do next, pick up a pen and write.

Rouse Yourself! Why do You sleep, O Lord? Awake... Why do You hide Your face? (Psalm 44:23,24)

Triune God, I call to You for help trusting in Your mercy and love.

The Power of Potlucks

A "potluck" may seem like some outdated custom once practiced in rural areas in the distant past.

On the contrary, the potluck dinner–where people get together and each brings food to share– is going strong, especially in Austin, Texas.

The Austin Progressive Potluckers meet each month with a different activist group playing host. The aim is connecting people and at the same time, discussing timely issues, including ways to build peace. One month's meeting focused on bringing Jews, Palestinians and others together.

"We're changing the world, one dish at a time," says Potluckers founder Bruce Kravitz. "Food, conversation, cool people: You just can't beat the combination."

Be creative in the ways you connect with others.

His salvation is at hand...steadfast love and faithfulness will meet; righteousness and peace will kiss. (Psalm 85:9,10)

Prince of Peace, enlighten our efforts at conflict resolution.

In Defiance: a Requiem

Thirty-five thousand Jewish prisoners died in Terezin, a village in the Czech Republic that became a concentration camp during WWII. Amidst their slaughter, a group of prisoners shared a moment of supreme defiance.

Rafael Schaechter, a young conductor, convinced his fellow prisoners to learn Verdi's *Requiem* and form a chorus. "We can sing to the Nazis what we can't say to them," he told them.

Even as prisoners were deported, Schaechter worked to teach the Latin score about God's wrath and human liberation to his campmates. One day, the group was asked to sing during a visit from SS officials including Alfred Eichmann.

There they stood, singing the powerful Latin words of the *Dies Irae:* "The day of wrath... What trembling there shall be when the Judge shall come. Nothing shall remain unavenged."

Few lived to tell the tale.

(God) will repay according to each one's deed. (Romans 2:6)

Show us, loving God, how to live with dignity at all times and everywhere. Show us how to speak out against injustice.

Age is but a Number

Unlike some folks who claim to be 39 well into their 40s and 50s, Tracy Chapman is enjoying her 40s and looking forward to the future.

The singer-songwriter, hit it big at 24 with her debut album, which won four Grammys in 1988, including Best New Artist. She says, "Success so early on taught me...that it's important to take time off to learn new things and be exposed to new experiences."

She is actively involved in various charities and causes, including voter registration. "We need to give democracy a chance by participating in it," Chapman says.

We can lose ourselves in success as easily as in despair. The important thing is to remember that it's a wide open world full of new things to learn and people to meet. When was the last time you took time off to learn something new? You just may surprise yourself in the process.

The heavens are telling the glory of God; and the firmament proclaims His handiwork. (Psalm 19:1)

Lord, may we never tire of discovering the wonders of Your world and sharing them with others.

The Value of Gratitude

Retired physician Robert Rento went to Nepal with other medical volunteers to give his time and talent to needy children. He returned with something of value–the gratitude of people.

A physician for 45 years, Rento traveled with a team from Interplast, a non-profit organization providing free reconstructive surgery for children in developing countries.

Conditions for the visiting medical team weren't ideal, according to Rento. There were power failures, limited supplies, long hours and blistering heat. But there were few complaints. He believes the professionals were inspired by their patients "often two or three in a bed, with gratitude as their only expression."

The Morang Cooperative Hospital gave their guests a "certificate of gratitude."

Saying "Thanks," showing appreciation, seems like such a small thing, but it isn't. It can mean the world.

Be thankful. (Colossians 3:15)

Inspire me, Holy Spirit, to be grateful for Your gifts.

A Well for Precious Water

We are constantly being urged to drink more water for good health. People in developed nations have ready access to water. That simply isn't true in many other countries. Geography and poverty can both create problems.

When missionaries arrived at Holy Family parish in Fiji a few years ago, they discovered that water was a problem for everyone in the area. Few homes had running water. A well that would have benefited thirteen families had been begun, but was abandoned due to lack of funds.

Rev. Diego Rojas asked for government help and encouraged families to work together. Muslims, Hindus, Anglicans and Catholics labored shoulder to shoulder. In time they were rewarded with clean drinking water.

It's easy to take water for granted when you have it. But for too many it's still a matter of life and death. Think about that the next time you turn on the faucet.

They did not thirst when He led them through the deserts...He split open the rock and the water gushed out. (Isaiah 48:21)

Merciful God, help me imitate Your compassion and reach out to assist those who need what I have in abundance.

Eleanor Roosevelt at Val-Kill

After the death of President Franklin Roosevelt in 1945, his widow, Eleanor Roosevelt, centered her life at Val-Kill, her cottage in Hyde Park, New York.

Allen Freeman writing in *Preservation,* says Val-Kill Cottage is as "plain and unaffected" and as "complex and contradictory" as was Mrs. Roosevelt.

At Val-Kill, the shy and down-to-earth Roosevelt warmly entertained everyone from important political figures to her grandchildren. There, she answered letters, wrote columns, speeches and books. She championed international human rights, spoke against McCarthyism and advocated civil rights at home.

Eleanor Roosevelt thought that her life showed "that one can, even without any particular gifts, overcome obstacles that seem insurmountable if one is willing to face the fact that they must be overcome."

Your talents are many and varied. Put them to use. Today.

To each is given the manifestation of the Spirit for the common good. (1 Corinthians 12:7)

May we recognize that we all have talent and then put it to good use, Lord of all.

Philanthropist's Gifts Keep Giving

When Paul Burns, advocate for the homeless, embarked on his Salt of the Earth ministry, he was not seeking recognition or reward. His aim was to help the homeless men, women and children he encountered daily in Bergen County, New Jersey.

Imagine his shock when he was awarded $50,000 as a result of a philanthropist's generosity and vision. Burns took the top prize in 1998 in the Russ Berrie Award for Making a Difference, which honors men and women dedicated to community service and helping others.

He used the money to feed the hungry (including having barbeques at local parks so that homeless people could get to know one another), to help homeless children and to provide clothing and shelter. Now, years later, Burns' efforts have not stopped.

It's great to help others, especially when it becomes your way of life. Make it yours.

The measure you give will be the measure you get back. (Luke 6:38)

Lord, thank You for the opportunities to serve others. In doing so, help me find a deeper appreciation for others' needs and what I can do for them.

A Call from the Heart

The ringing telephone sounds throughout Gladys Keene's apartment. The octogenarian widow looks forward to this weekly phone call from her best friend, Ruth Porter. For five years they've talked on the phone as if they've known each other forever. Yet the two women have never met.

"It just makes you feel good to know you're not alone," Keene says, "that somebody out there cares about you."

Porter started Salt Lake City's Telephone Reassurance Program by making a phone call. Since the first call, more than 350 volunteers have helped 375 elderly people form new long-distance friendships each day. There is even a spin-off home-visit program involving hundreds of others.

"It's wonderful to think that my little idea has touched so many lives," says Ruth Porter. "A little kindness and a telephone go a long way."

A little idea and a little kindness—what could you do with them?

**Kindness is like a garden of blessings.
(Sirach 40:17)**

Divine Father, with You by our side, we know we are never alone.

All Stressed up at Work

One out of every four Americans has been driven to tears by the stress of work. One in eight has called in sick because they were too stressed out to work. What can you do about it?

A number of authors on the subject recommend therapies from deep breathing, to thinking calming thoughts, to listening to soothing music during the work day.

One company's stress management consultant offers "hug therapy" to anyone having a bad day. At another, you can scratch behind the ears of Merlin, the stress management director. He's a white Maltese dog who belongs to the chief executive.

Perhaps the simplest solution to stressful jobs is to remember that work and life are not one and the same.

Do not live to work. *Work to live.*

And, enjoy your weekend!

There is nothing better for people...than...to enjoy themselves. (Ecclesiastes 8:15)

Carpenter of Nazareth, may my life always be a healthy balance of work and leisure.

Rights of Women–and Girls

In Genesis, women are created in God's image and likeness. Powerful and influential women are celebrated throughout the Bible.

Yet in the United States and other industrialized nations in the twenty-first century, women's rights and freedoms are too often defined for them; their abilities, denied or denigrated; their lives, circumscribed.

Remedy this injustice. Remind women and girls that they have the right:

- to resist gender stereotypes
- to express themselves
- to be economically independent through interesting work
- to have self-confidence
- to be safe both in their homes and outside
- to take risks, strive freely and take pride in success
- to accept and appreciate their bodies

Respect your sisters and brothers. Respect yourself. And expect to be respected.

I commend to you our sister Phoebe, a deacon of the church at Cenchreae. (Romans 16:1)

God, who asked Mary of Nazareth to bear, raise and teach Jesus, remind women and girls of their dignity and worth.

Turning a Gnat into a Cat

His first idea for a comic strip, "Gnorm Gnat," didn't fly. "I thought bugs were funny, and nobody else did," says Jim Davis.

But his next effort, a cat, clawed its way easily into the hearts of readers around the world. In fact, Garfield is as popular today as he was when he first pounced onto the pages of newspapers 25 years ago.

Why do so many go crazy for this fat, lazy and sometimes surly feline? Davis feels it's because Garfield offers something for everyone–sight gags for the little kids, an attitude for teens, and a struggle with weight and exercise for older folk.

Davis won't be walking away from his cranky cat any time soon. "I want to write the one gag that makes the whole world laugh," he says. "I haven't done it yet. That keeps me going."

And that seems to be purr-fectly all right with comic readers everywhere.

Be joyful. (Psalm 68:3)

I am filled with joy, Father, as I behold the glory of Your creation.

Trumpeter for Civil Rights

Walter Fuller, a jazz trumpeter who played with bandleader Earl Hines in the 1930s, died in 2003 at age 93. He had had a long and well-respected career as a musician.

He used his talent and influence in the San Diego music scene to promote civil rights. Fuller often protested nightclubs' seating policies that segregated black and white patrons. He managed to change the listings in the local musicians' union chapter, which had separated whites and blacks. In 1952, he became the first black director on the local union board.

If you're passionate about a cause, you can make a difference anywhere. Find the courage and conviction to express your views. You may be surprised at the impact you have!

For freedom Christ has set us free. Stand firm, therefore, and do not submit again to a yoke of slavery. (Galatians 5:1)

Lord God, help me see that the world needs my intelligence, beliefs, efforts to improve. Don't let me leave the hard decisions and challenging work to others.

When It's the "Other Guy"...

Here are some perhaps familiar ideas about how we look at ourselves and at others:

"When the other person acts that way, he's ugly. When you do it, it's nerves.

"When she's set in her ways, she's obstinate. When you are, it's just firmness.

"When he doesn't like your friends, he's prejudiced. When you don't like his, you're showing good judgment.

"When she's accommodating, she's apple-polishing. When you do it, you're using tact.

"When he takes time to do things, he's slow. When you take ages, you're deliberate.

"When she finds fault, she's cranky. When you do, you're discriminating."

If you want others to give you the benefit of the doubt, be ready to extend the same courtesy. It's the human thing to do.

Father...forgive us our debts, as we also have forgiven our debtors. (Matthew 6:9,12)

Abba, remind me that You expect us to get along and to love one another.

Mommy Matinee

"Shush." Many parents with small children rarely go to the movies because of that one little word, not to mention the comments that sometimes accompany it.

But on Tuesday mornings, almost 40 Loews movie theater lobbies around the country are filled with strollers, infants and toddlers and their parents. The Reel Moms program lets parents bring their children to the movies without worry.

From 10 a.m. until 11 a.m. it's bit of a free-for-all playtime for the kids with music, games and other activities. Meanwhile, moms and dads make friends of their own.

"It's a great way to meet other moms," says Helen Lloyd. "I moved here from London…and already have a bigger community of moms than I did there."

When life feels overwhelming, keep an eye out for some "playtime" of your own. And remember, you are not alone.

Wine and music gladden the heart, but the love of friends is better than either. (Sirach 40:20)

Father, bless all new parents and their children.

Solitude for the Soul

The writer Eugene O'Neill, one of America's most celebrated dramatists, won four Pulitzers and the 1936 Nobel Prize for Literature.

Although generally regarded as an East Coast writer, O'Neill lived in the San Ramon Valley, east of San Francisco for many years. His Spanish-style sanctuary that he named Tao House provided the intensely private O'Neill with the solitude and peace he craved as he crafted some of the most memorable scenes in the American theater.

Solitude does feed the soul. Give yourself the gift of it whenever possible. Whether it's a long bath or a quiet walk, even fifteen minutes of solitude can refresh your spirit.

In quietness and in trust shall be your strength. (Isaiah 30:15)

Jesus, I will take time each day to restore my spirit, to commune with You, in peace and solitude. But even when I am busy, or with others, let me always abide with You.

A Mother's Devotion

Mary Brown never intended to be foster mother to more than 100 children. In 1947, when her then 19-year-old son was about to leave home, she thought she'd like a little girl. She and her husband James decided to become foster parents. Soon after the little girl arrived, social services called to say the child's sister also needed a home.

Over the next 53 years Brown cared for 128 foster children, earning her the United Negro College Fund and the Washington Child and Family Services Office Lifetime Achievement Awards.

"When I found out people didn't want their children," she says, "I couldn't believe it. Whenever...children needed a home, I just said, 'okay.' " Mary Brown's lifetime of service came from her generosity and love of children.

When you generously follow your dreams and deepest convictions, wonderful things can happen!

**Those who are generous are blessed.
(Proverbs 22:9)**

Spirit of God, give me the clarity to know my mission and purpose in life, that I may fulfill the Father's will.

The Power of a Good Letter

When was the last time you wrote a letter to right a wrong or to offer your thoughtful opinion about a problem?

Many people fail to write letters or e-mails that either offer praise or constructive criticism because they don't believe it will do any good. But the founder of The Christophers, Rev. James Keller, M.M., knew that decision makers are more susceptible to public opinion than is generally realized and that just a few good letters can influence them.

All it takes is a little time, confidence and these tips from Father Keller to make your letter a good letter:

- write as if to a friend
- be constructive
- be specific
- be brief without being curt
- make your point but don't repeat it
- be yourself, writing as you talk
- offer positive suggestions, not just complaints

Take heart-and take up your pen.

Take courage. (Haggai 2:4)

Holy Spirit, may my words build up, not tear down.

Oops... Mmm... That's One Fine Cookie

Chocolate chip cookies are relative upstarts in the cookie world. Ruth Wakefield of Whitman, Massachusetts, first created them in 1930, by accident.

The Wakefields ran an inn called Toll House opposite a tollgate on the Old Boston-New Bedford turnpike. One day, she was making butter drop cookies and substituted a chopped up chocolate bar after discovering she was out of nuts. Instead of completely turning the cookie chocolate as she assumed it would, Ruth Wakefield was happily surprised to taste the first chocolate chip cookies.

They were a hit at the inn, and soon word of Toll House Cookies spread across America– along with its recipe.

Things don't always turn out as we expect. Don't be afraid to venture into uncharted territory. The next thing you try just might be a wonderful discovery.

Do not fear or be dismayed.
(Deuteronomy 31:8)

Holy Spirit, grant me the courage to follow Your gentle guidance.

A Commuter's Dream Cruise

Commuting easy for you? Hardly, according to most workers. But some suburban New Yorkers board a Hudson River ferry service, where it's not just about getting to work, it's about the people.

The Haverstraw-Ossining ferry hasn't been ferrying passengers for very long, but a camaraderie has developed among the "ferry people" that is rarely seen among suburban commuters.

Every morning, riders say "good morning," inquire after family members and take an occasional dig at the straggler for whom the ferry returns to the dock.

"We're more like a family," says regular rider Mary Devine, who's taken the ferry since its first run. "When I was out of work, people asked about me and when I returned, they greeted me like a long lost friend."

Throughout our lives we encounter opportunities to develop relationships with others. Keep that in mind. Your commute and life could be the better for it.

Faithful friends are sturdy shelter. (Sirach 6:14)

Holy Trinity, help us to make the most of each opportunity to connect with others.

Pig Gig

Dale and Lisa Siebrecht count seven generations of farmers in their combined family backgrounds. Despite their knowledge and commitment, however, they came perilously close to losing their Iowa family hog farm during the 1990s.

The Siebrechts decided to try one last strategy, signing on with a consortium of about 100 other independent family farmers who were growing Berkshire hogs for export to Japan. The moist and flavorful pork sells at nearly twice the price of the pork produced by factory farms; enough for the Siebrechts to stay in the business they know and love.

Have you been treading water lately, maybe even losing ground in an area of your life? Whether in your employment or in a relationship, consider taking a risk. Even a slight shift in your approach may do the trick.

Think things through. Then take action.

"Children, you have no fish, have you?" ..."No." ..."Cast the net to the right side of the boat, and you will find some." (John 21:5,6)

Where are You calling me to innovate, Creator?

R-E-L-A-X!!!

"Frantic families equal fragile families," says University of Minnesota Professor of Marriage and Family Therapy, William Doherty.

Yet there may be penalties for putting loved ones first. Leaving work on time can mean added pressure to finish projects and please the boss. And if children don't have a variety of extra-curricular activities it can hurt their chances of admission to certain colleges.

Yet many families think the effort is still worthwhile. Some Ridgewood, New Jersey, parents began Ready, Set, Relax! The BaRosses, for example, limit their daughters' after school activities. They themselves leave work on time. There's a weekly themed dinner at home followed by board games. Or they eat at a restaurant and then see a movie. Free time together is a priority.

We talk about family values and say that the family is the foundation of society. But are we as individuals, co-workers, employers and a nation nurturing every family?

Make the family your personal priority.

Do not wear yourself out to get rich; be wise enough to desist. (Proverbs 23:4)

Abba, bless each and every family.

It's Never too Late to Be Great

The next time you're feeling as if time has passed you by, consider these inspiring facts:

Writer Laura Ingalls Wilder published her enormously successful *Little House in the Big Woods,* the first of her eight-volume series, when she was 65 years old.

Lillian Carter, mother of President Jimmy Carter, joined the Peace Corps at age 68 and served for two years in India.

Jenny Wood-Allen of Scotland completed the London Marathon in 11 hours and 34 minutes. She was 90.

There are fewer limits to what each individual can accomplish, regardless of age, than we usually admit. Don't limit yourself. And don't let others limit you either.

Daughter, your faith has made you well; go in peace. (Luke 8:48)

God in Heaven, inspire me to live courageously, fully.

Shhhhhhh!

Don't just do something, sit there!

Jim McGinnis calls this admonition an upside-down insight. One of the topics he considers in his book, *A Call to Peace,* is "prayerful and careful" listening. He discusses how a quiet heart, in tune with the promptings of God, can lead to better listening abilities with others.

"Attentive silence before the Spirit who breathed creation into being enhances our attentiveness to all around us," he observes.

McGinnis cautions that learning to sit before the Lord in silence does not come easily. He began with ten-minute sessions that gradually lengthened as he became more comfortable with the practice of centering prayer. "I began to trust that this truly was not 'wasted time,'" he says, "even when I would start daydreaming or falling asleep."

McGinnis says a centered self is not self-centered but rather tuned outward as well as inward.

Invite the Lord to stay with you.

The Lord is in His holy temple; let all the earth keep silence before Him! (Habakkuk 2:20)

Show me the riches found in emptiness, Spirit of Holiness.

Care Package for Further Study

"As a college student, I love my independence," says Karen Langley. But, "at times—I admit it—I need my parents."

Langley polled her peers to find practical ways parents can give a boost to their youngsters away at college. She advises sending care packages. "Even the smallest packages means a lot, especially around exam time," she says. She once got a Valentine's Day gift from her mom, an envelope stuffed with "love messages" from her younger siblings. Homemade food is also always welcome.

Telephone calls from mom or dad can be the best cure for homesickness. During those calls, Langley says, don't be stingy with the advice. "We appreciate that you don't want to interfere, but don't hesitate to share your words of wisdom," she says.

"Not all our crises require a road trip by concerned parents," observes Langley, "but we want to know you care."

Everyday let your loved ones know you care.

Love one another with mutual affection.
(Romans 12:10)

Teach me Your ways, Father, so that I may love as You do.

A Picture of Harmony

Looking for something interesting to do one weekend around Sydney, Australia, Robert Billington went to Shark Island to photograph a swimming race. While waiting for the competitors to finish, he spotted a boy standing at the water's edge holding a prosthetic leg, looking for someone.

When his father emerged from the water, hopping on one leg with the assistance of another swimmer, the boy ran to him, beaming with pride. They all walked up onto the beach together to the sounds of applause and cheers from onlookers and swimmers.

"It wouldn't have mattered if he'd won or finished last," Billington says. "It was such a good thing to see a warm...relationship between father and son, and people helping each other."

To overcome one's disability and to go on with life is a challenge. To do so with the assistance of family and friends is a blessing.

Beloved, let us love one another, because love is from God; everyone who loves is born of God and knows God. (1 John 4:7)

Lord, bring us closer to You and closer to each other.

Dare to Dream

When Paola Del Favero set out to open a café on an empty lot next to her New Jersey home, family and friends told her she was, well, crazy. Two years later, Del Favero, her business thriving, has expanded into catering.

Consider these steps to your own personal success.

Write down your desires. On paper, they become more concrete.

Take baby steps. Every mini-milestone will come with a surge of confidence.

Build a support system. Surround yourself with those who will get and keep you moving. Tell the naysayers that you're in the market for cheerleaders *only*.

Don't be afraid of failure. As Talane Miedaner, author of *Coach Yourself to Success,* put it: "If you shoot for the moon and end up in the stars, that's not such a bad thing."

Making the most of God's gift of life is your gift to Him.

What shall I return to the Lord for all His bounty to me? (Psalm 116:12)

Fill me with courage, Father, to do what is right and to do all I can.

The Man Who Paints the Ponies

When the Paragon Carousel on Nantasket Beach in Hull, Massachusetts, celebrated its 75th anniversary, at least half of its original horses looked just the way they did on their first ride–thanks to James Hardison.

Spending over a decade on the task so far, the artist has restored more than 30 of the carousel's original 66 horses and has begun work on one of the two chariots. Repairs are made only with original materials–wood, glue and dowels. Hardison strips the paint down to the original coat so he can document and then recreate the original 1928 colors.

Hardison's daughter, Louise, once told a friend who asked where her father was, "My daddy lives at the carousel." Everything in life is a work in progress, even the fantasy world of the carousel.

Be willing to take time and trouble for things that matter.

Not to us, O Lord...but to Your Name give glory, for the sake of Your steadfast love and Your faithfulness. (Psalm 115:1)

Bless the work of my hands, Lord.

From Paralyzing Loss to Action

Monica Gabrielle's husband of 28 years, Richard, was crushed under a marble wall on the 76th floor of the south World Trade Center tower. She describes it, in her anger, as being "squashed like a cockroach."

At first, she lost her trust in human beings and could not leave her home. Then, with other victims' families, Gabrielle and Sally Regenhard began the Skyscraper Safety Campaign. The Skyscraper Safety Campaign asks why the towers collapsed so quickly, why more didn't escape and why the emergency communication systems did not work properly. "Somebody failed," Gabrielle says, and "needs to be held accountable."

The Skyscraper Safety Campaign won passage of the Construction Safety Team Act in October 2002. The law commits the National Institute of Standards and Technology to investigate building disasters and gives the Institute subpoena power.

Joining with others to prevent future disasters is a constructive way to heal after an horrific loss.

Unless the Lord builds the house, those who build it labor in vain. (Psalm 127:1)

Abba, remind all those who design and construct buildings to put safety first.

Land of Deprivation

Imagine not being able to find medical care for yourself or your sick child. In Tanzania there is only one medical doctor for every 25,000 people; whereas the U.S. ratio is one for 400. And the African nation's neonatal mortality is among the highest in the world.

Rev. Doctor Peter Le Jacq, M.M., who has served in Tanzania for over a decade, says the solution to the country's healthcare crisis is success "one patient at a time."

And hope is on the way. Tanzanians, relying on their own resourcefulness and the coordinated efforts of Maryknoll (Catholic Foreign Mission Society) and others in the United States, are establishing medical schools and forming alliances with U.S. universities and companies to secure financial aid, textbooks and supplies.

Crises that seem insurmountable can be resolved by persistence, creativity and initiative. How can you apply these qualities to a problem, now?

Bear fruit with patient endurance. (Luke 8:15)

When I am feeling weakest, Christ Jesus, help me find my courage, creativity and persistence.

Words of Wisdom

True words of wisdom are timeless. They never go out of style.

Throughout history there have been people who shared their insights with others. Lin Yutang wrote about both ancient Eastern and modern Western beliefs in his 1937 book, *The Importance of Living*. Scaled down to a succinct three points, his message as adapted by David Wallechinsky and Irving Wallace in *The People's Almanac* is:

- Be passionate in your love of life and appreciate its small pleasures.
- Keep a child's heart. Don't be afraid to be happy.
- Have the courage to be you.

Right now, take a minute, or even three minutes, to ponder the meaning and the message behind these words. In what ways do they apply to you? Try to put these ideas to work. Life is a great challenge. Meeting the challenge will be a great reward.

Wisdom gives strength. (Ecclesiastes 7:19)

Holy Spirit, grant me wisdom and the courage to act on it.

The Store that Sells Futures

Writer and educator Ned O'Gorman wanted to help give poor children a better chance in life by offering them a better and broader education.

In 1966, he turned a decrepit storefront in New York City's Harlem into a children's library and, two months later, into a school. This was the first of his efforts. Today three Harlem brownstones house a school that offers a fine education, from pre-kindergarten through eighth grade. O'Gorman exposes the children to the kind of education and to the culture usually reserved for the children of wealthy suburbanites, including French and Chinese lessons, and plenty of Mozart.

Many graduates have gone on to private schools and then to a variety of careers.

We have so many opportunities to do good in our lives. And the more we look for them, the more we'll find.

Train children in the right way, and when old, they will not stray. (Proverbs 22:6)

Teach me Your ways, Lord, that I may know how to bring hope to a waiting world.

Feeling Guilty about Work?

Plagued by unnecessary guilt on the job? Author Joe Robinson asks you to consider your likely reaction to this scene: you're driving when you suddenly notice a police car in your rearview mirror, lights flashing, siren wailing. Would you...

- feel flushed, certain you've acted illegally?
- calmly keep driving, certain you did nothing wrong?
- start preparing an alibi about your broken speedometer?

There is a difference between appropriate, genuine guilt and irrational, excessive guilt.

Says Robinson, "Mix hard work with a healthy sense of self-respect and you'll have more time for yourself."

While it's good to work hard at your job, it's also important to have a life outside of work. The demands of your job shouldn't overwhelm time with family and friends or time for community projects and favorite activities.

Strive for balance in all things.

As far as the east is from the west, so far He removes our transgressions from us. ...the Lord has compassion. (Psalm 103:12,13)

Thank You, Merciful Savior, for forgiving me. Help me to forgive myself.

Angel in the Palm of My Hand

After years as a stay-at-home mom, Peggy Bazyk, needing some extra cash, decided to return to work as a school crossing guard.

For the most part, the experience was positive. She enjoyed the bright faces of the students, and liked talking with their parents. There was, though, a downside, dealing with disrespectful children and rushed, rude parents.

One particularly bad day was made worse by pouring rain. "What was I thinking?" Bazyk wondered. Just then a car pulled up, the window rolled down and a woman reached out and pressed something into Bazyk's hand, saying, "Thank you for all you do."

As the car continued on, Bazyk opened her hand to find an angel pin. "That small act of kindness lifted my spirits for the rest of the school year," she said.

It is sometimes the tiniest gestures that can make the biggest difference for someone in need.

Clothe yourselves with compassion, kindness. (Colossians 3:17)

This day, Father, show me the joy amidst the difficulty, the light in the darkness. Help me share Your light with others.

More Thoughts on Happiness

We all want to be happy all the time. That would be ideal. But the reality is that happiness is a sometime thing. Happiness seems to go as quickly as it comes. Still, there are at least three qualities of happiness that are universal.

First: Your happiness comes, or doesn't, from the choices you make. Advice from others may be helpful but your choices of career, marital status and address, among others, are yours and yours alone to make.

Second: You alone can define your happiness. Pop culture and various groups equate happiness not only with your career, marital status and address, but also with your suit or dress size, financial situation, age, popularity, and so on and on. What makes you happy?

Third: Happiness is not a spectator sport. Have meaningful relationships with others. Enjoy your daily work. Make each day count. Pray often, as and when you are able.

Walking with God, begin your search for happiness today.

**Happy are those who find wisdom.
(Proverbs 3:13)**

Holy Spirit, in You may I find peace and joy now and in eternity.

The Churchills of Where?

Everyone knows who Winston Churchill is. He's the great leader who brought Britain through World War II. He's one of the most important figures in European history. He's the picture of English statesmanship. So it's only natural, of course, that his mother was born in...Brooklyn?

It's true. Jennie Jerome, who would later become Lady Randolph Churchill, was born at 197 Amity Street in Cobble Hill, Brooklyn, New York. Many might find that surprising, but the confusion doesn't end there.

A building at 426 Henry Street, also in Cobble Hill, bears a plaque that claims the building to be Jenny's birthplace. In reality, the plaque marks her uncle's home, where her parents stayed until shortly before her birth.

Avoid taking anything for granted. Not everything is as you expected.

You will do well to be attentive. (2 Peter 1:19)

Lord, help us to keep an open and clear mind, and to learn and seek things for ourselves.

Sock It To 'Em

Jim Bradley was among those who, in the 1960's, noticed unsettling changes in the land when coal companies began strip mining.

According to Amy Rawe of *Hope* magazine, "Strip mining tears open the earth and releases underground springs, causing the mountains to weep brown streams into the creeks and rivers below."

Bradley decided to take action on behalf of the rural Tennessee region he called home. He founded Save our Cumberland Mountains, a grassroots organization to fight the coal companies in court. Today the group has grown from 13 members to almost 2,500. It has fought irresponsible strip mining and logging practices, pesticide drift, economic inequities and social ills.

"We figured it out as we went along," Bradley says. "We'd try one direction, and if that didn't work we'd go in another. Nobody can whip you if you keep moving and don't give up."

When you are trying to do good, never give up. Never give in.

Take courage; I have conquered. (John 16:33)

Fill us with the fortitude to move mountains, Lord of all.

Everest and Gratitude

How do you express your gratitude to people who have helped you get to the top of the world?

In 1953, it took 350 Nepalese Sherpas led by Tenzing Norgay, to guide Edmund Hillary and other Westerners up Mount Everest from April 13 to May 28. They brought 1.5 tons of supplies to "Camp IX" at 27,900 feet. From there, Hillary and Norgay continued to the top. They reached Everest's 29,035 foot summit at 11:30 a.m. on May 29, 1953.

Sir Edmund says that later as he built "a close relationship with the Sherpas" he realized they lacked what "we just took for granted." He decided to remedy that by raising their standard of living and helping them get an education.

"My most important projects have been the building and maintaining of schools and medical clinics for my dear friends in the Himalaya and helping restore their beautiful monasteries too," says Sir Edmund Hillary.

Offer your appreciation daily to God and your neighbors.

Do not neglect to do good. (Hebrews 13:16)

Father, remind me to express my gratitude in deeds and not just in words.

Vigil by the Watchfires

On every May 30 since 1987, rows of fires have burned atop the Palisades along the Hudson River's west shore. These watchfires are lit at midnight and burn until dawn on the traditional Memorial Day, and are then refueled at dusk to burn again until midnight.

Veterans from the Vietnam Veterans of America (VVA) of Rockland County, New York, build these fires according to the military regulations and specifications of the 1700's, when similar fires burned to warn General Washington of British troop movements.

According to the VVA, these vigils by the watchfires are "for our fallen brothers, our patrol that has still not returned, and the patrols of past wars back to our country's first soldiers who fought along these shores."

Whether by keeping vigils by watchfires or by keeping alive a memory in our hearts, those who are lost remain forever with us. Let us honor their memories today and every day.

In the memory of virtue is immortality. (Wisdom 4:1)

Father, bless all veterans and comfort those who mourn all those who never came home.

Speaking of Hope

"Hope," wrote poet Emily Dickinson, "is the thing with feathers, that perches in the soul, and sings the tune without words, and never stops—at all."

History is filled with people who held on to hope.

Ludwig van Beethoven composed most of his music during the years of steadily worsening hearing loss.

Abraham Lincoln failed in business twice and was defeated in elections nine times! One of the few times he did succeed, he became America's 16th president, helping to end slavery while preserving the Union.

The next time things look pretty grim, just remember that history is filled with the hope-filled tales of those who kept their dreams soaring, and never stopped believing.

Hope that is seen is not hope. ...But if we hope for what we do not see, we wait for it with patience. (Romans 8:24-25)

Take my hand and let me cling to You, Jesus. Then no harm will come to me.

A Life of Conservation

Richard Pough died at 99 after a long active involvement in conservation.

Born in Brooklyn in 1904, Pough graduated from the Massachusetts Institute of Technology. By 1932, he owned a camera shop in Philadelphia and set out to explore an area known as Hawk Mountain. Appalled to find hundreds of dead hawks killed by hunters and simply left to rot, he photographed the carcasses and started a publicity campaign to end the killings.

In what became a model for his future conservation campaigns, the founder of the Nature Conservancy encouraged a philanthropist to buy 1400 acres of the mountain to protect the habitat. He also spread the conservation message by, for example, arranging discussions with leaders of garden clubs.

One person can make a difference in so many ways. Consider what's important to you and your neighbors and then do something positive to help your cause.

Good sense wins favor. (Proverbs 13:5)

Inspire us, Holy Spirit, to live sparingly, lightly on this earth, our home.

Making Like DiMaggio

In the summer of 1941, millions of Americans were gripped by a raging fever. Every day they stopped whatever they were doing to find out if New York Yankee slugger Joe DiMaggio had kept alive "The Streak"–getting a base hit in what turned out to be 56 consecutive games.

DiMaggio and his "streak" gave Americans something different from the war news coming from Europe. He became a national hero the likes of whom is needed even today, according to DiMaggio biographer Richard Ben Cramer. "I think there's still a great hunger in the country for somebody to look up to."

Heroes may still be found in the world of baseball, Cramer suggests. But no matter what the playing-field–classroom, board room, office, kitchen, laundry, hospital room, workshop or outdoors– any time you step up to the plate in life, you have the potential to score for the greater good of all.

Wisdom is as good as an inheritance...the protection of wisdom is like the protection of money...wisdom gives life to the one who possesses it. (Ecclesiastes 7:11,12)

Enlighten us with Your strength and wisdom, Blessed Trinity.

Not-So-Famous Freedom Fighter

When most of us think of the civil rights movement, Rosa Parks and Martin Luther King come to mind.

But Shirley Bulah Stamps? Yet her parents' 1954 fight for her right to ride a school bus was an integral part of the landmark court case that ended school segregation.

Stamps was just eight years old when her parents tired of driving her two miles to a black school in a nearby Delaware town while a bus passed their home each day on its way to a white school.

The Bulahs sued and won. For the first time, a segregated white school was ordered by a U.S. court to admit black children.

Individuals make a difference every day, sometimes quietly and without fanfare. Often, their impact is far-reaching and long lasting.

You have neglected the weightier matters of the law: justice and mercy and faith. It is these you ought to have practiced. (Matthew 23:23)

Jesus, help me work for equal justice under the law for all.

With Kindness

Theodore Isaac Rubin wrote, "Kindness is more important than wisdom, and the recognition of this is the beginning of wisdom." With this in mind, here are suggestions for those times when you must criticize someone:

- See yourself as a coach or teacher who is trying to help the other person progress.
- Demonstrate that you care sincerely about the person's success
- Pick the right time.
- Do not appear rigid and pedantic; avoid "shoulds."
- Stress that you want the person to improve; not that you want to see your ideas in practice.
- Show how the person will benefit from your suggestions.
- Make your suggestions specific.

A little kindness can make a difficult situation more bearable for all involved.

**Kindness is like a garden of blessings.
(Sirach 40:17)**

Give us Wisdom, Holy Spirit.

Raising Happy Children

Love and discipline are important to raising happy and secure children according to Dr. T. Berry Brazelton. The noted pediatrics professor and writer continues, "The one thing children need more than anything is a close-knit, loving family. Parents who can be really available are investing in their youngsters' futures as well as their own." He says, "when your baby gurgles and smiles, gurgle and smile back."

In addition to loving interactions, which over time create a special familial bond, discipline is also needed. "Discipline is not punishment," writes Dr. Brazelton, "it's teaching a child where and how to stop...a child who is not disciplined does not feel loved."

Parents should try to spend time alone each week with each child. Both actions and attentiveness convey to a youngster the message: "you matter." In the process, children will learn that others matter as well.

Pray for parents. The future of the world depends on them.

Every year his parents went to Jerusalem for the...Passover. (Luke 2:41)

Lord, give parents the wisdom and strength to guide their children to healthy maturity.

Easy as a Walk in the Park

New York's Washington Square Park is a popular public space for tourists, local college students and native New Yorkers. Few of them, however, are likely to know that they're sharing their sunny day in the park with a strange and varied past.

Washington Square Park was once a potter's field. According to imprecise accounts, there may be anywhere from 15,000 to 25,000 people, many of them slaves and yellow fever victims, still buried under the park. It's claimed that when the park was turned into a military parade ground during the mid-1800s, practicing troops often found their cannons' wheels caught in the ruts of graves that had collapsed under the weight above them.

Just a quick glimpse into the history of a place many wouldn't think twice about offers an interesting, unexpected past. Try to look at everyday things in a new light. You might be surprised by what you find.

**Observe carefully what is before you.
(Proverbs 23:1)**

Heavenly Father, help us to see the things we wouldn't normally see.

Hope-Filled Marriage

Hope is a critical ingredient in happy marriages. Why? According to the University of Denver's Center for Marital and Family Studies, we work harder at tasks when we are hopeful.

Sally Stich, writing in *Woman's Day* magazine, says of her own marriage: "Even in the worst times, I always hoped we could find a way to work things out. And so far, we have." She offers some additional traits of happily married couples:

- They make time to dream about their future.
- They have fun together.
- They think of themselves as we, not I or you.
- They applaud their partner's efforts to change annoying habits.
- They try to do things the other person likes.
- They confess when they're wrong and grant forgiveness when asked.

Easy to do? No. Worth the effort? Absolutely.

Let marriage be held in honor by all. (Hebrews 13:4)

Jesus, inspire us to imitate the faith, hope and charity of Your family.

A Reason for Hand Folding

True or false: as long as people have been praying they've done so with hands folded. False.

The custom of folding our hands in prayer dates to medieval Europe. Folded hands, a sign of a vassal or serf's obedience to a feudal lord, became a sign of obedience to God's will. And in some cultures, India for example, clasped hands are a sign of reverence.

People in the ancient world, in fact, prayed with their hands held aloft. For example, the Psalmist speaks of "the lifting up of my hands" (Psalm 144:2) as does St. Paul: "Pray lifting up holy hands." (1 Timothy 2:8)

Whether folded or raised, it is right that our hands, indeed every fiber of our beings, praise and thank God.

Let my prayer be counted as incense before You, and the lifting up of my hands as an evening sacrifice. (Psalm 141:2)

For all the blessings You've given me, Lord God, I raise my hands and voice in prayerful praise.

A Shining Example

Every Tuesday and Thursday, Albert Lexie rises at 5 a.m. and takes two buses to the Children's Hospital of Pittsburgh where he makes his rounds, shining shoes for $3.

And every Tuesday, he visits an office building near the hospital to hand over his shoeshine tips, gifts from customers and contributions to the hospital's Free Care Fund.

Since he started this routine in 1981, Lexie has given some $90,000 to this fund which helps pay for medical care for pediatric patients regardless of their families' ability to pay.

Lexie's shoe-shining career started almost 50 years ago, when he was 15 and made his first shoeshine box in a high school shop class. Watching an annual telethon that benefited the hospital planted the seeds of his idea for helping young patients.

We can all be philanthropists if we just think about creative ways to aid the charities that matter to us.

The righteous are generous. (Ps. 37:21)

Today, Spirit of Love, in all the chaos, help me find my way to You.

Images of a Haunting Past

Painful memories haunt Japanese-Americans who lived in the United States during World War II. Racial prejudice and fear of another Pearl Harbor attack led President Roosevelt to sign Executive Order 9066 in February of 1942.

Approximately 120,000 people of Japanese descent, mostly U.S. citizens, were removed from their homes and businesses in California, Arizona, Oregon and Washington to internment camps.

One of these was the Minidoka Relocation Center in Southern Idaho, home to nearly 13,000 Japanese-Americans, many of them children. Now called the Minidoka Internment National Monument, a number of one-time detainees have gone back to visit. Memories remain vivid. They recall the surrounding barbed wire, the guards and the watchtowers. Still, some said reliving those painful years would help them find peace.

War leads to suffering for so many people, in so many ways. Work for peace built on tolerance, respect and justice.

Blessed are the peacemakers, for they will be called children of God. (Matthew 5:9)

Jesus, Prince of Peace, guide our efforts for world peace.

Accounting for Trees

How much is that oak down the block worth?

The New York Neighborhood Tree Survey, a City Coalition project, examined 322 trees and determining the net worth of each.

"A healthy, growing tree is essentially a pollution-eating device and a mini-air conditioner," said David Nowak, a project leader from the Forest Service. The Survey found that the average tree has a value of $3,225; the most expensive, $23,069 and removes $34.33 worth of pollutants from New York's air each year.

The Survey hopes to illustrate the importance of trees by putting their worth into dollars. "Maybe with a real, hard dollar value on street trees, people will see them as more than just street furniture" said landscape architect Matthew Arnn.

We can easily forget the value of the mundane, of creatures, of Creation. Look at the world around you and remind yourself of its worth.

God made to grow every tree that is pleasant to the sight and good for food, (also) the tree of life...and the tree of the knowledge of good and evil. (Genesis 2:9)

Lord, help us to see the worth of all around us.

What's in a Word?

Sometimes a single sentence can capture a life lesson that resonates with most of us. Consider the following gems:

First, a Swedish proverb: "God gives every bird his worm, but He does not throw it into the nest."

Then, from Archbishop Fulton J. Sheen, "Each of us makes his own weather, determines the color of the skies in the emotional universe which he inhabits."

Finally, the words of Dr. Smiley Blanton: "To be happy, drop the words 'if only,' and substitute instead with 'next time.'"

You may have noticed that each of these phrases has a common thread. We are all given many opportunities to succeed in numerous ways throughout our lives. How we embrace those opportunities is the all-important second half of the equation.

Human success is in the hand of the Lord. (Sirach 10:5)

May I never play the victim, O God, but rather embrace Your offerings.

Preserving the Past

The Ephrata Cloister, once a German Protestant monastic community near Lancaster, Pennsylvania, is now an historic site.

In the 17th century, Germans fleeing religious strife settled in Pennsylvania. Here, the Quaker William Penn had decided there would be freedom of religion.

The immigrants brought German folk culture and language, vernacular architecture, applied arts and a strong work ethic with them.

Visitors today can sample this rich culture in choral concerts, illuminated manuscripts known as frakturschriften, and in such architectural elements as A-shaped chimneys, dormer windows, low ceilings to conserve heat and a tile-roofed outdoor bake oven.

Nowadays when many things are mass-produced and found worldwide, it's good to see a place that values and preserves a unique past.

An appreciation of history is vital for understanding the present.

(God) has made everything suitable for its time. (Ecclesiastes 3:11)

Help me appreciate the past even as I live now and move into the future, Almighty One.

What Whets Your Whistle?

Ever pay too much for something? Benjamin Franklin did and he never forgot it.

In *The Man Who Dared the Lightning*, historian Thomas Fleming recounts Franklin's life. He tells one story of how a seven-year-old Franklin was given some coins by a visitor. Not long after, he saw another boy blowing a whistle and, deciding he had to have it, gave all his money for the whistle.

Fleming goes on, "Ben played the whistle all over the house, enjoying it until he discovered that he had given four times as much as the whistle was worth. Instantly, the whistle lost all its charm."

As an adult, when Franklin noticed someone neglecting family or business obligations for popularity, or giving up friendships to pursue wealth, he would say, "He pays too much for his whistle."

It can't hurt to ask yourself if you're paying too much for any whistles and what you're going to do about it.

**Godliness is valuable in every way.
(1 Timothy 4:8)**

Help me see myself with clear eyes, Dear Father. Help me spend my time and talents wisely and as You desire.

The Legacy of a Courageous Woman

Biologist Rachel Carson found that DDT, a pesticide, harmed human beings, wild animals, fish and birds.

Determined to inform the public Ms. Carson wrote *Silent Spring* in 1962. Both the manufacturers of DDT and the federal government said she was overstating the risks. But that didn't discourage this extraordinary scientist, who was already dying of breast cancer, from presenting her case before a U.S. Senate committee.

During the Kennedy administration a Science Advisory Committee sustained her research and conclusions. During the Nixon administration, DDT was finally banned.

Rachel Carson died in 1964. She once said, "It is a wholesome and necessary thing for us to turn again to the earth and in the contemplation of her beauties to know the sense of wonder and humility."

Have you experienced this wonder lately?

The One who prepared the earth...filled it with four-footed creatures...who sends forth the light...and it obeyed Him, trembling; the stars shone...with gladness for Him...this is our God. (Baruch 3:32,33-34,35)

Holy God, may we preserve Your earth, our home, for future generations.

Ice Cream for the Soul

While out to dinner with his family, Jimmy prayed: "God is good. God is great. Thank you for the food and I would even thank You more if Mom gets us ice cream for dessert."

Some patrons laughed, but one woman scoffed, "Asking God for ice cream! That's what wrong with this country. Kids today don't even know how to pray."

Well, Jimmy was quite upset until an older man reassured him that "a little ice cream is good for the soul sometimes."

Jimmy's mom bought the children ice cream at the end of the meal, and when Jimmy was served, he gave his sundae to the woman.

Kindness and understanding are good for the soul. A little ice cream on the side can't hurt either. We cannot possibly know how hard the road others walk.

Forgive, and you will be forgiven; give, and it will be given to you. A good measure...running over...for the measure you give will be the measure you get back. (Luke 6:37-38)

Lord, help us to refrain from pettiness and be gracious and kind to all.

Strategic Farming

Bradley and Louise O'Neal own Coosaw farms in South Carolina. About a quarter of their 1200 acres is devoted to growing 12 to 15 million watermelons a year. It's not an easy business.

Bradley explains that trucks move through the fields at about 10 miles an hour while the fruit is being picked at the rate of about 2 miles an hour.

"Your buyers are moving at 50 miles an hour and your labor is at 20," he observes. "You have to make sure they all come together at exactly the same point." Success means buyers purchase fruit that has been plucked from the fields about a day and a half earlier. A miscue results in wasted melons, an unhappy labor force and uninterested buyers. Coosaw Farms also grows soybeans, cotton, wheat, cabbage and corn.

Hard work can pay off, but not without careful planning.

We rely on the Lord our God. (Isaiah 36:7)

Give us the energy to work in concert with Your many blessings, Lord.

A Father's Best Gift

Parents generally want their children to have "the best," in so far as they are able. It starts with looking after their physical needs, but youngsters' minds and spirits need to be nourished as much as their bodies. That's why, for better or worse, the beliefs and attitudes of parents affect their children for a lifetime.

Historian Doris Kearns Goodwin talks about the importance of her dad's decision to overcome a difficult childhood to build a positive future for himself and his family. "What is clear is that at some point my father determined he would write the story of his life himself, rather than let it be written for him by his tortured past," says Goodwin. "And this resolve was the greatest gift he bequeathed to his children."

We need to understand our yesterdays and learn from them, but not at the expense of today. Remember that all children have a right to their own tomorrows.

I have set before you today life and prosperity, death and adversity....Choose life so that you and your descendants may live.
(Deuteronomy 30:15,19)

Heavenly Father, help us resolve to fulfill our lives in health and holiness, according to Your grace.

A Special Grace

Jay Walljasper loves watching his seven-year-old son, Soren, eat.

"He approaches his plate of food with something like awe," says Walljasper. "A smile breaks across his face and questions fly across the kitchen: What's this called? How do you cook that?" Soren's parents often notice he surreptitiously uses his hands to explore the texture and temperature of new foods.

"The joy of eating! That's what everyone seeks at mealtime," Walljasper proclaims. That concept, juxtaposed against the reality of busy families eating dinners reheated in the microwave or ordering at fast-food drive-thru windows, is jarring.

"The joy of eating has, in many ways, become a vicarious thrill," says Walljasper. He believes that mealtime feels unsatisfying to many not because of empty calories, but because we are starved for ritual and leisure and pleasure.

Says the doting father: "Dining with Soren offers a glimpse of Eden."

The Lord of hosts will make for all peoples a feast of rich food, a feast of well-aged wines, of rich food filled with marrow. (Isaiah 25:6)

Bless us, O Lord, and the bountiful gifts of food You bring to our tables.

Point and Shoot

Can a simple click make a difference?

Esther Cohen, executive director of Bread and Roses in New York City, thinks so. She has joined with Unseen America to amplify the voices of those who are often society's invisible.

Cohen told *New York Times* reporter Anthony DePalma that when cameras were given to a group of homeless people, some of them took photos of houses and apartment buildings "because that is what they never had."

DePalma also quoted a Chinese garment worker who said that taking photographs of her life made her feel "like a frog that jumped out of water."

Under the tutelage of professional photographers, the workers have captured the symbolic, the meaningful and the mundane. At the completion of each project, Bread and Roses exhibits selected photographs at a gallery exhibit.

Every one of us needs to feel that our lives have value. Let's also appreciate the worth of our neighbors' lives as well.

Better to be poor and walk in integrity than to be crooked in one's ways even though rich. (Proverbs 28:6)

Creator God, inspire us with new ways to empower others.

Dammed If You Do...

Beaver: A large, luxuriously furred North America rodent with two orange front teeth. Beaver: A tenacious hydraulic engineer and builder of lodges and dams. Beaver: Monogamous pairs have two to six kits (offspring) a year who live with them.

People in Knowlton Township, New Jersey, know a lot about these creatures. Beaver dams on local streams and lakes had been torn down or dynamited. Beaver families rebuilt them, over and over again. They flooded town land and blocked fire hydrant pipes. Earthen berms and pipes did not impede their engineering.

The town, located near the Delaware River, has finally capitulated to the beavers. Children are writing beaver songs and essays. The mayor's shirt bears a beaver image. June 21 is officially Knowlton Township Beaver Day (though the mammals are nocturnal).

Giving in to the inevitable can be a mistake, or the right thing. Life is full of decisions. Make the best ones you can.

Pursue peace. (Hebrews 12:14)

Remind us, Creator, that we are stewards, not masters, of Your creatures, Your Earth.

Fostering the Future

Fernando Rosales might have dyslexia.

The preteen would most likely have been diagnosed with the reading disorder, but his working-class immigrant family couldn't afford the nearly $2000 it would cost to have him properly evaluated. Their health insurance wouldn't cover the expenses, either.

That didn't mean Fernando was on his own, however. He had a closely-knit web of support, including Florence Molloy, his guidance counselor, and Thomas Moran, a high school senior who volunteered at Fernando's high school.

Together they've worked with Fernando and increased his grades dramatically. The little boy no longer hates math. And they've discovered that when someone reads a test to him, Fernando tends to score 30 to 40 points higher than on those when he's left to struggle by himself.

Sometimes talent needs to be fostered with a little understanding and kindness. How can you help those around you?

Have pity on us and help us. (Mark 9:22)

Lord, help us to help those we can, when we can.

Tastes So Sweet

You will leave two neighboring stores in Belmont, North Carolina, with a smile—and not just from the food. Cherubs Café and Gifts & Candy Boutique are both run by the Holy Angels Corporation, a Sisters of Mercy ministry.

The Holy Angels Corporation was founded to meet the needs of mentally-challenged children and adults in residential environments. As the children grow into adulthood, the sisters provide vocational training.

One of the adult kitchen helpers, Lorraine, is mentally retarded. She began with the most basic chores. Now she prepares salad and sets the tables for lunch.

The café and boutique prove that mentally challenged individuals, with supervision, can overcome their disabilities. Regina Moody, president of Holy Angels said, "It helps us...educate others that people with disabilities can work."

How can you make someone's life easier?

The compassion of human beings is for their neighbors. (Sirach 18:13)

Lord, today help us make another's life a little sweeter.

Finding Solace through Nature

Ground Zero: the locale of the September 11th catastrophe is burgeoning with signs of renewed life. Weeds have emerged out of the charred ground and a sparrow is nesting in a nearby sycamore tree, building its nest out of detritus.

The U.S. Forest Service organized the Living Memorials Project with a million dollars from Congress. They are helping 20 communities to remember, through nature.

Family members and survivors in some New Jersey and New York neighborhoods were given money to plant trees in tribute to the deceased. Nadia Murphy, who lives in an area which lost many people, said, "This is a place for us to come together...to help each other heal."

Plant a tree, a garden. They are symbols of healing and remembering that through the ashes, new life will burst forth.

May their memory be blessed! (Sirach 46:11)

Remind us, loving God, that the life and death of every person has meaning to each one of us.

Why Forgive?

Most people probably think of forgiveness in terms of spirituality. However, more and more researchers are finding that the ability to forgive colors a person's attitude and overall health.

Everett Worthington, the executive director of A Campaign for Forgiveness Research, a non-profit group which promotes studies in this field, says, "Chronic unforgiveness causes stress. Every time people think of their transgressor, their body responds."

Both the immune and cardiovascular systems can be hurt, but the good news is that people can learn to forgive, with positive results, including less stress, anger and depression.

Psychologist Suzanne Freedman believes that it's important to remember that forgiveness does not imply acceptance of the hurt; nor does it mean forgetting what happened or reconciling with some-one who is still inflicting pain.

If you have not been able to forgive someone, think about it again: not just for that person's sake, but for your own welfare.

Forgive your neighbor. (Sirach 28:2)

Gracious God, thank You for forgiving me. Help me forgive others.

Stress + Boredom + $ = Teens at Risk

From smoking to drinking to taking drugs, teens are more likely to try these dangerous activities when they are stressed, bored and/or have ready cash.

Almost 2,000 youngsters aged 12 to 17 were surveyed by Columbia University's National Center on Addiction and Substance Abuse. Teens with two or three of those characteristics are three times more likely to get into those bad habits than young people who do not exhibit them.

Joseph Califano, the Center's president, says, "High stress, frequent boredom and too much spending money are a catastrophic combination for many American teens." But, he continues, "How parents act...their attitudes about drugs, and how engaged they are in their children's lives will have enormous influence."

The cost of ignoring risky behavior is too high a price for any family to pay. Nothing replaces the time and interest that parents give their children.

Children, obey your parents. (Ephesians 6:1)

Abba, give parents strength, wisdom and love to do their best for Your children.

Hair Today, to Love Tomorrow

Kevin Berg, a graduate of Carlsbad High School in New Mexico, decided he wasn't going to let his long hair wind up in the wastebasket after his regulation Army haircut.

Instead of waiting for the Army to give him a buzz cut, 18-year-old Berg got his hair cut a few weeks early and donated the hair to Locks of Love, a nonprofit organization that provides hairpieces to children across the United States who have lost their hair, usually from disease or chemotherapy.

The organization uses donated hair to create high quality wigs. The wigs help restore self-esteem and confidence in the children and helps them face the world and their peers.

"This is the first time we've had someone donate their hair before enlisting," said Berg's Army recruiter Sgt. Jose Hernandez.

And the children served by Locks of Love are most certainly glad for their new locks.

There are always ways to turn the simplest actions into opportunities to help others. Do something extra today.

The Lord...repays mortals according to their deeds. (Sirach 35:22,24)

Bless me with a generous heart, Master. Today, help me answer a call for help.

Children: A Well of Optimism

Many parents pride themselves on instilling a sense of right and wrong, good manners and obedience in their children. Doubtless, these are noble values and add to a youngster's strong character.

But what about optimism? As children get older and enter their early teens, one of the first hurdles they face is belief in their own worth and abilities, and in the future.

One way parents can help youngsters grow into optimistic adults is by helping them weather trials and errors. "Hopeful children are positive about the future because they have overcome problems and succeeded in the past," says a clinical psychologist.

Encourage your children to work through, not avoid, life's challenges. You'll be filling them with a lifelong well of optimism and hope.

Encourage one another. (1 Thessalonians 4:18)

Lord of all, the world can seem hopeless at times. Lift up my spirit so I can see the glorious hope inherent in Your Word.

Blues Monkee

Peter Tork rose to fame in the 1960s as part of the musical group and television sitcom *The Monkees*. Before he ever sang about "The Last Train to Clarksville," Tork fed off his mother's jump and swing records. So when the train pulled out and *The Monkees* went off the air, he returned to his early influences, including the blues.

What does a sixty-plus former pop star have to say about singing the blues? "You don't have to be a black sharecropper to play the blues," Tork said. "But you do have to overcome the...disease...(of) 'otherizing' everyone else, distancing yourself from the humanity of anyone who isn't you."

The message is in the music for Tork.

All of us on this earth share a common humanity. Let's treat one another as family rather than dividing into "us" and "them."

There is one God, the Father, from whom are all things and for whom we exist.
(1 Corinthians 8:6)

Heavenly Father, we are all part of Your family. Help us recognize that means we are all brothers and sisters, too.

Weaving Webbed Wisdom

Eight tiny ducklings, with their hen and drake, picked blueberries, wondered at the places where waves met the land, moved along crooked paths and learned straight-as-an-arrow decency.

In 2003, at age 88, Robert McCloskey, the man behind these magical birds, died at his home in Maine. His narrative and artistic talents had made him a cherished guest at bedtime story-telling for generations of families. The Ohio native who penned so much children's literature had, in fact, first wanted to become a musician, then a mechanic.

Make Way for Ducklings, his second book, was first in fame. In it, McCloskey told of Mr. and Mrs. Mallard and their quest to find a safe place to raise their young. In doing so, the author gave readers a duck's-eye view of Boston, as well as messages about the caring, loving relationship between parents and children.

Share literature with your family. Most of all, share yourself.

Love one another deeply from the heart. (1 Peter 1:22)

Lead me along the right path, Father. Show me the way to serve You best.

Bob Hope: Thanks for the Memories

Centenarian and comedian Bob Hope died in July of 2003. He had created fond memories for millions, including American service men and women on duty overseas.

According to Mort Lachman, Hope's head writer, director and producer for years, the entertainer loved getting laughs and would go almost anywhere for them.

Having grown up in poverty, the famous comic was cagey when it came to money. "If I had $500 million, I wouldn't go to Vietnam—I'd send for it." But Hope did go to Vietnam and many other places as well. In 1943, after his first performance for the GIs, *Time* put him on its cover.

Over the years, the troops, lonely for a touch of home, proved to be a great audience. "The civilian audience was tough and unreasonable," Hope joked in his memoir. "They wouldn't laugh at the jokes unless they were funny."

Will you be remembered fondly as a bringer of joy?

Eat your bread with enjoyment, and drink your wine with a merry heart. (Ecclesiastes 9:7)

God, bless those who bring joy and laughter to others.

Free Gifts

Stumped by what to get for a birthday or a holiday? Or perhaps the problem is a shortage of cash. Well, here's a list of virtually free ways to give a gift that comes from your heart.

- **Call.** Think of someone who isn't expecting to hear from you, and make the call that says he or she is in your thoughts.
- **Read.** Read to a child or perhaps an adult–the driver on a long car trip, a friend with impaired vision or your spouse at the end of a long day.
- **Visit.** Making the time to just be with someone could be a greater gift than you could imagine.
- **Drive.** Give someone a ride to church services or to a store.
- **Clean, cook.** These good deeds shine brightest when unexpected.
- **Pray.** This is a gift you can offer anytime, anywhere.

Just as you did it to one of the least of these who are members of My family, you did it to Me. (Matthew 25:40)

May all I do today, Loving Lord, be a reflection of Your faithful, steadfast love.

Military Dolphins

When you think of combat veterans, do you often think of dolphins?

Programs to train and use dolphins in combat situations have been adopted by several countries over the past few decades. The intelligent sea mammals have been used by navies to guard military installations, locate and chase off enemy divers, find mines and other buried objects and even plant tracers and locators on enemy ships.

While it may seem like an unusual–perhaps even absurd–idea, even the US Navy has a military dolphin program, known as NRAD. When the dolphins become too old, the Navy often "pensions" them out, placing them in homes at sea parks or sanctuaries.

Help can come from the most unlikely places. Always be open to it.

Your God is the one who helps.
(1 Chronicles 12:18)

Creator of all, help us to recognize the willingness to help of all around us.

Hot Dogs and Hostility?

For many Americans, the Fourth of July is a time of fireworks, flag-waving and barbecues. But after September 11, 2001, celebrating the Fourth has changed for Americans living overseas.

Whereas many ex-patriots once proudly and publicly displayed their national pride, with the rise of anti-American sentiment during the occupation of Iraq, many celebrated quietly or not at all.

Denis Campbell, an American living in the Netherlands, refuses to hide the "fierce love of country" his own father, a naturalized U.S. citizen from Jamaica, instilled in him.

Campbell has spoken out at rallies and appeared on Dutch television in an effort to understand the Dutch perspective as well as to "serve as a face and voice for my homeland."

Working to preserve the rule of law and promote justice for all is another expression of patriotism.

How do you express your patriotism?

Cease to do evil, learn to do good; seek justice, rescue the oppressed, defend the orphan, plead for the widow. (Isaiah 1:16-17)

Holy Spirit, protect and preserve our liberty.

Answering God's Calls

Diane Dunne felt God prompting her to leave a lucrative career in the cosmetics business to become involved in a lay ministry. During a gospel rally in a park, a tattered homeless woman named Alaska asked her: "What do you know about what it's like to be homeless?"

Shocked and strangely moved, Dunne began returning regularly to the park to bring Alaska and other homeless people sandwiches. She even accompanied Alaska to her "home"—a filthy space with a 10-gallon steel drum for a toilet.

Dunne next decided to found Hope for the Future Ministries, which ministers to Manhattan's impoverished seniors, the homeless and unemployed, street kids, substance abusers and single mothers. "Most people we deal with have given up on man and God," says Dunne. "My greatest satisfaction is when I see someone come to Jesus and his or her life is totally turned around."

How do you get your satisfaction?

As you did it to one of the least of...my family you did it to Me. (Matthew 25:40)

How may I serve You this day, Lord? Teach me. Guide me.

Thelma's Solution

Octogenarian Thelma Harrison is still going strong. During the past 15 years, she began changing the lives of her fellow Norfolk, Virginia, citizens.

"In this community, many mothers don't have a great deal of education," she say. "They need help." She decided to provide that help.

Harrison did a little fundraising, found two student teachers and began a free, six-week summer program for children ages three and four. The children learn their ABCs, how to count to 100, how to tie their shoes and other basic lessons. When it is time to begin kindergarten, they are ready.

At the same time, Harrison has gotten to know the families of these children, mentoring and being there for them.

Here's a fine example of how an individual's one-on-one caring can go a long way to improve the future for those in need.

Blessed are those who hunger and thirst for righteousness. (Matthew 5:6)

Jesus, never let me give up in despair; help me find simple solutions.

Angry Eating

Ever found yourself so angry that all you did was eat and eat? Thomas Wadden, M.D says that "people who swallow their anger feel, for whatever reason, that they can't express it, so they resort to food."

Family problems led a Michigan teacher, mother and wife to use food to handle her anger. "I felt I had no control over anything," she recalls. She ate sweets, became angry with herself and ate more.

In *Woman's Day*, Sally Shannon suggests instead…

- Avoid sarcasm and insults which invite a counterattack.
- Start small.
- Say, for example, "I feel really annoyed/upset when I see you haven't…" and then mention what hasn't been done.
- Talk things over after you've calmed down.

Anger is a healthy, God-given emotion. Express it appropriately, so that it doesn't harm you—or others.

(Jesus) said to her, "Daughter, your faith has made you well; go in peace, and be healed." (Mark 5:34)

Thank You, Lord, for helping people acknowledge their anger and express it well.

Runaways Can Ride Home

To the local police, he was just one more runaway.

But when the boy's body was found, Richard Voorhees, a New Jersey police chief, felt the anger of the youngster's father—and his own sense of guilt and frustration. Voorhees thought about runaways, wondering how they'd get back if they found themselves far away and broke. And he had an idea.

Voorhees approached an interstate bus line which agreed to provide a one-way trip home for those under 18. Today, the "Home Free" program is offered by Greyhound Lines through the National Runaway Switchboard (800-621-4000). 1,000 youngsters a year take a ride that gets them off the streets and back to their families.

Because one man wanted to do more than simply regret a mistake, thousands of families have had reunions.

Good can come from the failure, pain or loss you have experienced—if you make it happen.

Lord, You are our Father; we are the clay, and You are our potter; we are all the work of Your hand. (Isaiah 64:8)

Holy Jesus, look after our children and help us give them the love, acceptance and forgiveness they need as they mature.

Shaping Up Your Soul

Life can resemble a circus act: we juggle work, children, spouse, house, friends, relatives, health, community involvement–not to mention caring for ourselves. Where does God fit in?

Spiritual direction is believed to have begun in the fourth century when Christians sought the wisdom of a desert amma or abba (mother or father). Then, as today, spiritual directors, by listening and asking questions, can lead people to see God's direction in their lives.

Benedictine Sister Josue Behnen says God needs to be in the middle of it all. The St. Cloud, Minnesota, spiritual director tries to help others "see how God is trying to love them into wholeness and happiness." She walks with others "so they can be comfortable to be real with God."

Spiritual direction is, then, like the safety net for the circus of life. Have some kind of safety net for your life. And be sure God is at the center.

Acknowledge the Lord, for He is good, and bless the King of the ages, so that His tent may be rebuilt in you in joy. (Tobit 12:10)

Walk with me, Holy Lord. Strengthen me with Your love.

Is Change Inevitable?

Could it be that some things aren't meant to change? Or at least not right away?

For instance, Bobby Robinson doesn't plan to change any time soon and many think that's a good thing.

According to one news report, Robinson is "perhaps the longest-lasting black business-owner on (or just off) West 125th Street" in New York City. The 85-year-old Harlem record-shop owner, music producer and World War II veteran has seen a lot of changes over the years. "The big stores just took over," says Robinson, now surrounded by a number of chain stores.

But inside his shop are wonderful pictures of Robinson posing with such notables as Gladys Knight, Muhammad Ali, Fats Domino and James Brown. Robinson's musical memories are also part of the attraction for customers who respect his expertise.

We all know that change is inevitable. But isn't it nice to know that once in awhile it comes later rather than sooner?

I am the Lord; in its time I will accomplish it quickly. (Isaiah 60:22)

Help us, Divine Trinity, to understand what changes are necessary now, and which ones can and must wait.

The Future is Bright, and Tiny

During a stint at jury duty, MIT engineer Alan Epstein had a most unusual epiphany. Remembering a question posed to him once by a U.S. Air Force official, he thought: how difficult would it be to build a jet engine the size of, say, a coffee cup?

Could a tiny turbine be built using the approach perfected by computer-chip makers?

In that jury room, Epstein thought up preliminary ideas for what eventually became the microturbine. "The future is small," says Epstein, hinting that tiny machines could be the next big thing.

Where and when are you most inspired? Taking long walks? While driving or exercising? The shower?

Ideas can arise under the most unusual circumstances.

**To get wisdom is to love one oneself.
(Proverbs 19:8)**

Teach me, Lord, to find creative solutions to problems.

"O" My

Oprah Winfrey doesn't like to talk about her business. It's not that she isn't having a great time creating it. She sits at the top of an empire encompassing television, video production, film, and now *O Magazine,* the most successful start-up magazine in the history of publishing.

"The only time I think about being a businesswoman is now while I'm talking to you," she told Patricia Sellers of *Fortune.* "There's a part of me that's afraid of what will happen if I believe it all."

Winfrey went on to say that if she called a strategic planning meeting, staff members would fall out of their chairs laughing. She doesn't hesitate to confess that she can't even read a balance sheet.

It's clear that she follows her passions. "I don't care about being bigger, because I'm already bigger than I ever expected to be. My constant focus is on being better."

"Focus on being better"—that's a valid idea for anyone.

A woman who fears the Lord is to be praised. Give her a share in the fruit of her hands, and let her works praise her. (Proverbs 31:30-31)

May we be bold, Spirit of Wisdom, in our dreams and in our actions.

Raising Happy Kids

Conscientious parents and grandparents strive to provide the best environment in which to raise happy and healthy youngsters. Here are some ideas from *Reader's Digest*:

- **Have an involved Dad.** Sociologist Scott Coltrane found that children who do chores with their fathers are more cooperative at school. "They learn that everyone needs to do their part." It's enjoyable.

- **See green.** Since looking at greenery can be calming, put youngsters' beds or desks facing a window with views of grass, trees, or other foliage. If that isn't possible, "houseplants might also have some benefit," says Nancy Wells, author of the Cornell University study.

- **Stimulate children's' minds.** The *Reader's Digest* reports that children living in areas that spend money on the arts and recreation tend to be healthier. Go to parks at least weekly; museums, and zoos regularly.

And while you're at it, take time to be happy yourself.

Discipline your children while there is hope. (Proverbs 19:18)

Bless children with loving and conscientious parents and grandparents, Creator.

Those Long, Hot Summers

Who doesn't have at least one pleasant summertime memory?

There's something magical, and almost mystical, about summer. It represents a respite from rules, regulations, obligations and everything that restricts, even cold weather.

As adults, summer is often the season we remember as holding our childhood's dearest, fondest memories. Whether it was a special time at the seashore, a friend's cabin, a first kiss, travel to a special place or just playing stickball on a city street, summer memories last a lifetime.

Yet remembering the past can be bittersweet. How odd that our sweetest thoughts can often be shadowed by sadness. This paradox seems true about many circumstances. Life can be complicated, but if we trust God, we can always find our way.

Take My yoke upon you, and learn from Me; for I am gentle and humble in heart, and you will find rest for your souls. (Matthew 11:29)

Triune God, I pray for the wisdom to understand that life is complex, but the path to You is clear and easy to follow.

Table for Two—Twice

Lori Peikoff likes to tell the story of how her parents met in a busy restaurant in Manhattan. Her mother Deborah was engrossed in a used copy of *Great Expectations* and barely looked up when he asked if she'd be willing to share her table.

She did notice, however, when Lori's father, Joseph, a painter, sat down. At the end of the meal, Deborah wrote her phone number in the book and gave it to her dining companion.

It's a simple and charming story, save for one thing: Joseph lost the book. Heartbroken, he made several attempts to find Deborah, to no avail.

It was several months later, sitting in a crowded restaurant in Paris, that Lori's mother was again asked if she'd share her table. Looking up from her reading, she discovered that her new tablemate was again Lori's father, who had moved to Paris for his art.

Treasure life's surprises.

Lead a life worthy of the calling to which you have been called. (Ephesians 4:1)

Lord, help us to appreciate the surprises life offers.

Creating Success

Famous 19th century showman P.T. Barnum included in his autobiography some solid advice on achieving success. Here are the main points:

1.–Avoid debt. "There is scarcely anything that drags a person down like debt."

2.–Persevere. "How many...losing faith in themselves have relaxed their energies, and the golden prize been lost forever?"

3.–Whatever you do, do with all your might. "Work at it, if necessary, early and late...not leaving a stone unturned, and never deferring for a single hour that which can be done...*now.*"

4.–Depend on your own personal exertions. "No man has a right to expect to succeed in life unless he understands his business...learn(ing) it by personal application and experience."

Whatever our goals, we will never reach them without hard work.

Run with perseverance the race...before us. (Hebrews 12:1)

Holy Spirit, bless my efforts that they may serve Your will.

Final Vindication

At 10:18 pm on July 17, 1944, an explosion tore apart the U.S. Navy's Port Chicago, California ammunition depot killing 320 sailors of whom 202 were black enlisted men. Another 233 black "Bluejackets" were injured.

Three weeks later, 258 black sailors were told to load ammunition at Mare Island. They and their white officers had still received no special training in handling ammunitions. Traumatized by the previous explosion, they refused. Fifty were tried, convicted of "mutiny," and imprisoned.

Legal challenges maintained that the sailors were victims of prejudice by a segregated Navy. Although the convictions were upheld, the sailors were given honorable discharges in 1946. The Navy was the first service to end segregation.

One of the sailors, Freddie Meeks, was finally vindicated in 1999, when he received a presidential pardon. Through 55 years, Meeks had not lost hope. "I knew God was keeping me around for something," he said.

Patience and hope get us through even the bleakest times.

God said, "let us make humankind in Our image." (Genesis 1:26)

Holy Creator, help us, Your children, treat each other respectfully, equally.

Doors to Change

At 14, David Payamps was just another kid in a gang. "Luckily, I didn't kill anyone," he says.

Then he walked through the doors of Fresh Youth Initiatives, a tiny youth-oriented community service organization in New York City.

Now 22, Payamps has put in hundreds of hours of community service in his Washington Heights neighborhood in Manhattan. He has also led his own group within Fresh Youth Initiatives, and serves on its board of directors.

In December 2003, the former gang member graduated from Marymount Manhattan College. Says Payamps, "doing community service is a gift that opens doors for you."

And never closing off all the possibilities for your life can make a difference for you and for so many others.

O give thanks to the Lord...who remembered us in our low estate...and rescued us from our foes, for His steadfast love endures forever. (Psalm 136:1,23,24)

We give You thanks, Lord and Lover of souls, for Your healing, saving presence is never far from us.

Pretzels, Champagne–and Bookkeeping

The next time that you eat a pretzel, sip champagne or balance your checkbook, spare a thought for the monks who invented them.

Dom Perignon is a fine French champagne. It's named after the Benedictine monk whose experiments with grapes, fermentation and bottling techniques led to the bubbly drink that first enjoyed raves in the French court of Louis XIV.

Pretzels whose twists recall a monk's arms folded across the chest in prayer were first baked for Lent by monks who wanted to remind people to pray.

And that system of debits and credits you use to balance your checkbook–what's called dual-entry bookkeeping–was invented by Franciscan Luca Bartolomes Pacioli.

God gives us skills. Regardless of how we live, it's up to us to discover them and use them for the good of all.

He gave skill to human beings that He might be glorified in His marvelous works. (Sirach 38:6)

Inspire us, Eternal God, to do good things that give You praise.

Prayer in Motion

"I entered the circular path of the labyrinth in the retreat-center garden looking for answers to a conflict," says Melanie Bowden. "Within minutes, insight so overwhelmed my skepticism that I stopped in my tracks and gasped out loud."

Her experience is not unusual for those embracing the ancient tradition of labyrinth walking. Reporter Robin Cuneo walked one while researching an article on the subject and became such a fan she constructed one in her yard.

According to Cuneo, labyrinths are intricate patterns of winding paths leading to a central point. They are not mazes, meant to confuse, but paths meant to enlighten. Many are based on labyrinths built into the floors of European cathedrals.

Says new devotee Donna McCartney: "You can bring all your worries to God, and let Him take care of it all. That's what He does anyway, but this way is more inspiring."

Wherever you go, walk in God's presence.

Come to Me, all you that are weary and are carrying heavy burdens, and I will give you rest. (Matthew 11:28)

Show us new ways of being with You, Spirit of Truth.

Cricket Spitting Shenanigans

Those outside the pest control industry might expect the educational clinic of the New Jersey Pest Management Association to be a bit unusual. It's unlikely that many, however, would be prepared for the competition first held during its 56th annual meeting. Brown house crickets, which are about the size of watermelon seeds, were frozen, slightly thawed and then spit for distance by contestants.

"Because it's frozen, it makes it easier," said one contestant about the crickets. "They're not all squirmy."

The Guinness world record for cricket spitting is 30 feet, 1.2 inches. The first New Jersey champion spit his cricket 28 feet, 5.75 inches. He won a smiling metal cricket for his efforts.

Different groups of people have customs, activities and amusements that can seem unusual, silly or just plain strange. But if you make an effort to learn about others, while you might not want to imitate them, you'll certainly understand people better.

Acquire wisdom. (Sirach 51:25)

Holy Father, help us to appreciate all those around us.

Effecting Real Change

If you would like to join with friends, family and neighbors to create positive change in your community, consider both specific goals and overall ideals. Think things through—and keep thinking—as you proceed:

- recognize your strengths
- confront your weaknesses
- acknowledge what cannot be changed
- articulate your vision
- be realistic
- go beyond past animosity
- think strategically
- respect diversity
- use mainstream and independent media for publicity
- commit money, not just time and talent
- get to work

Nothing great was ever accomplished without unity, honesty, effort and wisdom. Pray for wisdom, now.

Give me now wisdom and knowledge.
(2 Chronicles 1:12)

Divine Lord, bless the efforts of all who strive to improve living and working conditions for Your people.

The Human Spirit Triumphs

John Merrick was born in 1862 with a rare genetic disorder that caused abnormal and crippling growths on his body.

The so-called "Elephant Man" spent years as a carnival exhibit as barkers exploited his misfortune for financial gain.

Fortunately, Dr. Frederick Treves, a London surgeon, met and befriended Merrick. He encouraged Merrick's love for reading and the theater. He also brought Merrick the company of caring friends who saw beyond appearances to the sensitive man beneath. Merrick lived the rest of his life supported and loved.

The late anthropologist Dr. Ashley Montagu, who wrote *The Elephant Man: A Study in Human Dignity,* believed this story was a triumph of the human spirit.

The influence of good people, he wrote, "never really fades...courage and integrity are among the supreme virtues of humanity, outlasting even death itself."

How do you use your influence for the good of others?

If we love one another, God lives in us, and His love is perfected in us. (1 John 4:12)

Jesus, enable us to live with courage, compassion and integrity.

Ready To Play But Not Able

Sue Sally Hale loved polo so much that for years before the gender barrier was removed she disguised herself as a man to play in tournaments

"I had my first horse at 3," Hale recalled. So by her early teens she was ready to compete with men. She started using mascara on her upper lip to create a mustache, wore extra large shirts and pulled her hair up under her helmet.

Hale persisted in trying to gain admission to the United States Polo Association. Eventually, with her determination and the efforts of her polo-world friends, the association admitted Hale as its first female member in 1972. By the time Hale died at age 65, she had had the satisfaction of seeing her daughters excel in the sport—as well as knowing that hundreds of women were members of the association.

To what lengths would you go to do what you love? Think about it.

Elijah said to Elisha, "Tell me what I may do for you, before I am taken from you." Elisha said, "Please let me inherit a double share of your spirit." (2 Kings 2:9)

Blessed Trinity, strengthen our resolve to pursue our loves.

Gathering Speed

One day Barry Farber took his four-year-old son on a bike ride. Having much shorter legs than his dad, the little boy had to work hard to get up the hills they encountered.

"If you want to coast when we're going downhill, you don't have to pedal," Farber advised his son.

"But Daddy," his son replied, "I want to keep pedaling so I can get up the next hill."

Farber was struck by his son's wisdom.

"When things are going well, and the going gets a little easier, we can't afford to coast all the way," he observed. "Don't neglect the little things," he said, underscoring the importance of taking advantage of momentum.

He continued the analogy: "We must begin pedaling again so we can get up the next hill."

To get where you're going, sometimes the most important thing you can do is to just keep going.

Out of the mouths of babes and infants you have founded a bulwark...to silence the enemy and the avenger. (Psalm 8:2)

May we always embrace the energy in our lives, and use it to Your honor and our good, Father of all.

Working for Peanuts

We've all heard stories of famous people who did not meet with immediate success.

Charles Schulz, creator of the comic strip *Peanuts,* was no exception. Enrolled in a course called "Drawing of Children," Schulz earned a C+. Yet he remained true to his calling and eventually sold some cartoons of children he dubbed "Li'l Folks" to the *Saturday Evening Post.*

"It seems beyond comprehension that someone can be born to draw comic strips, but I think I was," he once said.

He once wistfully told an interviewer that he would have loved to have had the talent of an Andrew Wyeth or a Pablo Picasso because he did not consider himself to be a true artist.

Still he said, "I can draw pretty well and I can write pretty well," he said. "I think I'm doing the best with whatever abilities I have been given."

What more can one ask?

These (who) rely on their hands and are skillful in their own work...maintain the fabric of the world and their concern is for the exercise of their trade. (Sirach 38:31,34)

Holy Spirit, inspire artists and all of us to use well the talents You have given us.

Something to Think About

Many people are uncomfortable talking about, even thinking about death. While this might be understandable, it can actually hinder us experiencing the here-and-now.

Dr. Elizabeth Kubler-Ross, the renowned psychiatrist and author of *On Death and Dying,* wrote, "It's only when we truly know and understand that we have a limited time on Earth —and that we have no way of knowing when our time is up—that we will begin to love each day to the fullest, as if it was the only one we had."

Just as we need to accept the mortality of our bodies, we ought to contemplate the immortality of our souls. Only then can we fully appreciate the wonder of the lives God has granted us. However, difficult and painful, or happy and successful any phase of life may be, it will pass. And one day, each one of us will exchange time for eternity.

The trumpet will sound, and the dead will be raised imperishable, and we will be changed. (1 Corinthians 15:52)

Remind us, Lord of Life, that You have made us for Yourself; to spend eternity in Your loving presence.

It's Not That Complicated

In 1960, four students at an all-black college in North Carolina decided to do something about racial discrimination. They took seats at a "whites only" lunch counter. In doing so, they essentially helped propel the civil rights movement to a new level.

Years after this landmark event, one of the protesters, Franklin McCain, remarked on the simplicity of their action. "Four guys met, planned and went into action," he said. "It's just that simple." Actually it wasn't that simple, at all–it took a tremendous amount of courage.

Taking positive action to make a change–whether in the world at large or inside yourself–starts by deciding to do it. If you want to pursue something worthwhile, think carefully, decide rationally and act courageously.

Be courageous and grow strong.
(1 Maccabees 2:64)

Help me find the motivation I need to make positive changes, Jesus, in me, my community and the world.

You Say Tomato...

It might interest you to know how a 'non-organic' or conventional food such as a tomato comes into existence.

First, the tomato is grown from a seed in a greenhouse with a solution of synthetic fertilizer. Then, it is transplanted to a fertilized field. After this, it is sprayed with fungicides and insecticides.

The tomato is picked while still green, then treated with ethylene to induce ripening, before being trucked to a store near you. Who ever thought so much went into growing a simple tomato?

Taking care of your health and your body honors Your Creator. Stay mindful of the food and other substances you consume. Remember that your precious body houses your eternal soul.

Your body is a temple of the Holy Spirit...which you have from God...you were bought with a price; therefore glorify God in your body.
(1 Corinthians 6:19,20)

Spirit of Wisdom, remind me of the importance of healthy living.

On Seeking Justice

On July 30, 1945, in the waning days of World War II, the U.S.S. Indianapolis was torpedoed and sunk by a Japanese submarine. Of the 1,996 sailors aboard only 316 survived the shark-infested waters before they were rescued.

In 1996, 11-year old Hunter Scott watched the movie "Jaws" and was intrigued by the scene in which that story was told. While doing research for a school project, Scott sent questionnaires to the survivors. All were outraged that the Captain, Charles McVay, had been court-martialed for the sinking. To deflect criticism of its handling of the situation, the U. S. Navy had apparently withheld evidence.

Scott began a drive to clear McVay's name and reveal the truth. Four years later, in October 2000 then President Bill Clinton signed a Congressional resolution exonerating McVay of wrongdoing.

It takes bravery to right a wrong. But think of Hunter Scott and do your best.

Never speak against the truth. (Sirach 4:25)

Give me the courage and commitment, Holy God, to seek and to speak the truth.

Comic Relief

Four-year-old Evan Petropoulos, hospitalized with a serious sinus infection, was giggling like a maniac. He'd just had a visit from Donna Mermel and her "humor cart."

For more than five years, Mermel's colorful cart, overflowing with neon-hued toys, smiley-face stickers and whimsical noisemakers, has rolled through the hallways of Advocate Lutheran General Children's Hospital in Park Ridge, Illinois. Mermel and her volunteers drop in to see kids with not too much to smile about and make them laugh.

Using humor to ease pain and help healing is no laughing matter to a growing number of doctors, nurses and other health care professionals. A small yet significant body of research, in fact, suggests that the ability to see life from the lighter side may be medicinal, increasing pain tolerance and bolstering the disease-fighting immune system.

The next time you're feeling under the weather, let a smile be your umbrella.

A joyful heart is life itself. (Sirach 30:22)

I am filled with joy, Merciful Savior, grateful for all the blessings You have sent my way.

Take the Air Conditioner, P L E A S E

After a woman had windows replaced in her home, she had a working air conditioner that didn't fit any of them.

So she called a couple of charities that usually accept such donations and was told to bring the unit in for donation. Both times the unit was rejected.

Desperate, she drove to a mall, cleaned out the car trunk except for the air conditioner and put a sign on it, "Free, working air conditioner…help yourself." Then she went shopping.

When she returned a card on the window read: "Dear Nice Person, Thanks so much! Our 16,000 BTU has been in the shop for 2+ weeks waiting for a compressor. I'm disabled and this is a blessing. Many thanks to you and yours–and the nice man who helped my nephew put it in our car. Best Wishes. Debbie."

She e-mailed her sister, "Can you believe how nice?!!!! It made my day. Divine intervention."

A generous person will be enriched. (Proverbs 11:25)

Jesus, it isn't easy to be generous, especially if we have known economic uncertainty. Heal us. Unclench our fists.

Growing through Crisis

The last thing most of us want to face would be a crisis. After all, it means a disaster or catastrophe, right? Well, not really.

"The true meaning of crisis...reminds us that the concept does not belong in the category of the negative–in fact, a crisis can be a very positive factor," says educator and theologian Rev. Eugene Hemrick. "The word belongs to a larger family of words–e.g. critic, critical, criticism and criterion. Each of these words is ultimately derived from the Greek word *krinein,* which means 'to decide', 'to be at a crossroad'. When properly understood, a crisis is an opportunity to make new commitments or bolster old ones."

We don't control everything that happens to us, but we always decide our attitude. Decide to be positive. Decide to cope with any and every crisis you face.

I will decide what to do. (Exodus 33:5)

Holy Spirit, show me the way through the difficult choices I must face each day. Show me the way home to You.

The Power of Love

"Before I came to Magdalene, I didn't have anything...I was a body with no soul in it. (Here) they just loved me and loved me...until I could learn to love myself," said Sheila.

Magdalene is a two-year recovery program for women with criminal histories of prostitution and drug abuse begun in 1997 by the Rev. Becca Stevens and a few volunteers from St. Augustine's Chapel on the campus of Vanderbilt University.

"It's based on an old model of community where your spiritual, physical and emotional needs are all being met in a safe environment," says Stevens.

Clemmie, a new grandmother with decades on the streets, says Magdalene "has allowed me to want to be a part of a community...It has given me self-esteem." Having been so loved, she now wants to share with others. "You know, I can't sing or nothing, but love, that's a great gift I got."

Love changes everything.

God so loved the world that He gave His only Son, so that everyone who believes in Him may not perish but may have eternal life. (John 3:16)

Merciful God, teach us how to love.

Raising a Posse, Cyber-Style

While Jason Eric Smith was a college student, he would support himself by restoring Macintosh computers and selling them on the Web. But when a con artist cheated him out of a sale, Smith's finances were thrown into complete disarray. Neither the Web firm nor the police were of much assistance.

In response, Smith turned to the online community. Other Mac users offered advice on how to use Internet resources to track the person who had cheated him. Some visited the address Smith had found and took pictures. Smith used this information to contact the local police, who used a sting operation to arrest the man who had cheated Smith and several other computer sellers.

Though none of them knew each other, Smith and his online posse were able to catch a professional con artist. Care for others and cooperation with them can do remarkable things.

My help comes from the Lord. (Psalm 121:2)

Lord, help us to do what is right, because it is right.

Reaching Out When Life's Caving In

Annie faced a Friday evening dragged down by life's trials: her five-year-old's school adjustment issues, her husband's business problems and her own struggles at work. Life seemed to be falling in on her and she wanted nothing more than to spend the weekend on her couch, watching movies on TV and eating cake.

Then the telephone rang. Her friend Cindy's sister had died suddenly and Cindy needed to talk. Immediately Annie invited her over; the two talked and cried into the early morning. The next day Annie drove her friend to the airport so she could fly home to her family. Then Annie spent hours cleaning Cindy's apartment, readying it for her friend's return.

In the midst of dishwashing and bed making, Annie felt her own life getting lighter. It seems as though reaching out—with help and hope—is the way to face life's difficulties when they start to weigh you down.

Help the weak, be patient with them all. (1 Thessalonians 5:14)

Bring hope to our days, Holy Spirit.

Simple Pleasures

As adults, sometimes just playing the simple games of our youth can help bind us together with old friends and family. Also, playing these games can help us recall those past years when life seemed more carefree.

For residents from Puerto Rico, Jamaica, Guyana, Trinidad or Cuba, dominoes were just such a game. And they are still a common summer recreation on the streets of certain communities.

"Dominoes have traditionally been a mostly male affair, the games often suffused with the boasting and bantering of a locker room," according to a New York Times story.

But women also participate and, have at times, predominated. For instance, Laura Jesurum is a local legend among those living in her working class neighborhood of Corona, New York.

Games, leisure, relaxation, are important for spiritual, mental and physical health.

Rejoice and exult with all your heart. (Zephaniah 3:14)

As I continue my journey to you, my Lord, please guide my steps. Help me enjoy simple pleasures.

Together to Success

Teamwork is one of those words that gets more lip service than practice–except at the biotechnology company where Myrtle Potter is the chief operating officer. "I truly believe that you can do absolutely anything with the right team focused on the right goal, all together working toward a common place."

Potter learned these lessons early. Growing up in a large close-knit African-American family, she knew what it was like to struggle for money. Still, her parents encouraged their children to use hard work, discipline and focus to achieve their goals. Everyone's needs were taken seriously, and all were expected to contribute. "We really did learn to sacrifice and give and really work as a team," Potter says.

Now, she believes its her mission "to help people grow, to help them achieve their greatest potential."

At work or home, we need one another.

Two are better than one, because they have a good reward for their toil. For if they fall, one will lift up the other...And though one might prevail against another, two will withstand one. (Ecclesiastes 4:9-10,12)

Blessed Trinity, it's so easy to concentrate too much on myself. Please open my heart to the needs of others.

Just Do Nice Things

When Dorene Simonds of Maryland was 18 years old, her car broke down in a desolate part of Texas. Stranded with very little money, she finally got hold of an old man with a tow truck.

While driving to the nearest town about an hour away, the two became engaged in an absorbing conversation. The next day, a shocked Dorene learned from mechanics that her car needed a new motor and that the repairs had been paid for by the older man.

He left her a note explaining his actions. Her kindness and conversation had simply motivated him to pay for the repairs. In return he asked that she continue to "just do nice things for other people."

Dorene continues the chain of kindness started so many years ago, "Every time I see someone in need I try to do all I can for them."

Be kind, and ask others to pass it on.

Do to others what you would have them do to you. (Luke 6:31)

Savior, inspire me to deeds of kindness.

Truly Seeing

"In a dark time, the eye begins to see," Scott Russell Sanders quoted Theodore Roethke after September 11. "In this dark time, what might we see that was hidden from us in the blaze of our prosperity?" he asks.

Sanders saw that suffering, unattended, breeds hatred and cruelty. "I realized as never before that our task as humans is to reduce the load of pain in the world, to alleviate suffering in everyone we meet, in every way we can," he says. "I had known these things as facts of the mind, but in the hours following the attacks, they became truths in my heart."

A professor at Indiana University, Sanders believes those "harrowing days have shown us that we possess enormous reserves of kindness, courage, wisdom, and restraint."

It is the challenge of every one of us to use God's gifts not only for our own benefit, but for our brothers and sisters, as well.

Let justice roll down like waters, and righteousness like an everflowing stream. (Amos 5:24)

May we honor those who suffered by keeping these truths alive, Loving Father.

Keep it Simple

"Wakefield, Michigan was a real-life Mayberry, right down to the barber shop, the soda fountain, and the big front porches," remembers Paula Spencer. She felt it was heavenly: playing at a lake near her grandmother's home, collecting rocks, and stopping in the library to read Nancy Drew books.

As a mom today, she has seen safety issues and urban sprawl interfere with the desire to create such an idyllic upbringing for her own kids. But she believes some elements of child rearing today should be re-examined. For one thing, many kids could use less structure.

One summer she sent her three children to a local day camp each day from 9 am to 3 pm. There were tennis lessons and arts and crafts periods to enjoy, along with swimming and more.

"Don't make us go back there," they begged her the next year. "There was no time to play!"

The streets of the city shall be full of boys and girls playing. (Zechariah 8:5)

Shake up our thinking, Lord; help us embrace simplicity.

Talk to Me

A group of 25 people, mostly strangers, discussing random thoughts and theories on a street corner is not a common sight in Manhattan. But because of two determined students and a hand-painted sign reading "Talk to Me," people from all walks of life started conversing.

"I believe that everyone...has something to learn from each other," said NYU student Bill Wetzel. With that in mind, Wetzel and his friend Elizabeth Barry spent a summer going from neighborhood to neighborhood in New York City to get New Yorkers talking. They discovered that everyone does have a story to tell, and that with a little encouragement, that story can be shared.

It's easy to forget that we are all individuals with histories, thoughts, feelings and ideas. Share yourself with someone today, and don't forget to listen in return.

Be patient. (James 5:14)

Father, give us the patience and compassion to listen to others and let us not be afraid to tell our own stories.

Those Long, Long Waits—"On Hold"

Most companies boast a stellar customer service and satisfaction record. Print and television advertisements trumpet: "The customer comes first."

Yet, it's not uncommon for customers to have trouble finding help when needed. Frustrating waits on hold, while trying to find help, are the norm. Electronic voices rather than a real human being are usually the service "person." Worse, some receive rude treatment or don't have their questions answered, no matter how long they wait.

What's a consumer to do? First, file a complaint with a consumer advocacy organization or the Better Business Bureau. Next, write letters to the company itself. Many firms especially in highly competitive industries, such as retail, do heed customer suggestions and complaints.

There is a right way to complain. Always be constructive.

Let your eyes be open and your ears attentive. (2 Chronicles 6:40)

Father God, help me realize that while I am only one person, I am important, I can make a difference.

Natural Intelligence

When rancher Fred DuBray sees bison roaming the grasslands of South Dakota, he sees a remarkable similarity between the herds and his people, the Cheyenne River Sioux.

DuBray believes the structure of Native American tribes on the plains was modeled after the buffalo herds that provided them with food, clothing and other necessities of life.

DuBray has been convinced since boyhood that restoring the buffalo to the plains would in turn, revitalize the health, culture and economic independence of his people.

Since then, he's worked diligently to expand bison herds on reservations, as well as assisting tribes in buying grassland acreage for the herds. And the bison herds have grown. "When the traditional lifestyle was disrupted, a lot of self esteem went down the drain too," he says.

What is vital to your cultural identity? Chances are, it is an integral part of what makes you unique. Celebrate your heritage.

Whose offspring are worthy of honor? Human offspring. ...who fear the Lord. (Sirach 10:19)

Spirit of Justice, I pray for tolerance and understanding in our world today.

100 Reasons Not to Make Lawyer Jokes

When attorney Andrew Moore was preparing to testify before a Congressional panel on the treatment of immigrant children who enter the United States without adult relatives or guardians, he turned to the lawyers at Latham & Watkins in Washington, D.C.

In fact, more than 100 lawyers at the firm have made refugee children the centerpiece of their *pro bono* legal work. They have Internet links to advocacy groups, immigration organizations and other lawyers who represent some of the nearly 5,000 unaccompanied children detained by the Immigration and Naturalization Service annually. Many children have fled forced recruitment as soldiers, laborers or prostitutes. The efforts of these lawyers has won praise from the American Bar Association and political leaders.

Benoit Jacqmote says his firm's work with child immigrants showed that "a big firm can wrap itself around a big project and make a difference."

A big difference, that is.

Do not despise one of these little ones...their angels continually see the face of My Father in heaven. (Matthew 18:11)

To those who cry to You, Lord, send hope; grant mercy.

A Contemplative Life

In her book, *Revelations of Divine Love,* Julian of Norwich tells us very little about herself or her life. In fact, she neglects to mention her own name. Her anchorhold, or cell-like room, was attached to St. Julian's Church in Norwich, England, and so she is known as Julian.

What the 14th century anchoress, or self-imposed recluse, does write about are her visions from God–even sin serves a purpose in God's plan–and her subsequent total dedication to a life of prayer and seclusion.

Today, many of us can't conceive of this level of dedication and devotion. But to Julian, expressing her love for God involved her entire life, to its very end.

How do you express your love to God and those dear to you?

Set me as a seal upon your heart, as a seal upon your arm; for love is strong as death, passion fierce as the grave. (Song of Solomon 8:6)

Jesus, remind me that love is more than a feeling. Help me appreciate the phrase, "I love you."

Angling for Her Truth

A few years ago, Judy Israel enjoyed nothing more than gathering with her Bridgewater, Connecticut women friends to play mah-jongg. Today she is more likely to be found in a boat at the crack of dawn, preparing for a long, hot day in the sun matching wits with bass.

Giving in to her passion for fishing, Israel turned professional in 1996. Although she's not likely to get rich in her chosen field, she has managed to break the top ten on the pro circuit, earning respect in the heavily male-dominated field.

According to the *New York Times,* for Israel to participate in a 3-day tourney can mean bringing along as many as 46 rods, hundreds of lures, extra hooks and lines, and both heavy and light rain gear. What she lacks in brute strength, she says, she makes up for in good technique.

What are you passionate about?

**Simon Peter said..."I am going fishing."
(John 21:3)**

Gracious God, we celebrate the many ways in which You fill our hearts.

Captive Kindness

Harry Nixon was held as a prisoner of war in Germany for several months during 1944 and 1945. He and his fellow POWs faced hardship, danger, injury and deprivation while they were held in Nazi camps, but they also found humanity.

"Meister," the camp boss, had himself been held by Americans as a POW during WWI. His positive experiences in American custody led him to treat his own captives as humanely as possible.

"He had been treated fairly by the Americans," says Nixon. "He remembered that, so he did his best to treat us fairly too."

That reciprocated courtesy led to unexpected good will. Returning to the scene of his incarceration more than 50 years later, Nixon sought out Meister's grave. Meister's son guided Nixon and his wife on a tour of the area.

Even in the worst of circumstances, humanity and kindness can make a lasting difference. How can you do that in your own life?

Pursue peace with everyone. (Hebrews 12:14)

Lord, help us to care for all, even when it is difficult or unexpected.

Getting A Second Chance

How would you handle a new lease on life?

At age 41, Venus Gines thought she was a healthy Latina about to start law school. Her world changed when she was diagnosed with breast cancer and lupus, an autoimmune disease.

"It was a very traumatic time," says Gines, the single mother of a pre-teen and a teen. "I made a will and arranged for the care of my son and daughter. Little did I know that God had other plans for me."

She promised God: "If you'll just give me these extra years, I'll use them wisely. ...I'll do everything possible to help my community."

Venus Gines has used the ensuing years to educate other Latinas by appearing on Spanish-language radio, conducting workshops, working with the American Cancer Society, and organizing culturally sensitive health festivals.

In similar circumstances, what would you change?

Remember your Creator in the days of your youth, before the days of trouble come. (Ecclesiastes 12:1)

Help us, Father, to use our time wisely, creatively, generously.

Just A Little?

The response to Fred Astaire's first screen test at MGM Studios left little doubt as to the potential talent of the performer hoping to make it into films. "Can't act. Can't sing. Balding. Can dance a little," the testing director wrote in a memo.

Astaire, of course, went on to star in dozens of movies. He and Ginger Rogers glided their way through films such as *The Gay Divorcee* and *Top Hat* and into cinema history as Hollywood's most famous dancing pair. Through the years, Astaire kept a copy of the MGM screen test memo in a frame over his fireplace.

The surest judge of your talent is yourself. Trust in your abilities.

Do not, therefore, abandon that confidence of yours; it brings a great reward. (Hebrews 10:35)

Spirit of Wisdom, help us to believe in ourselves and what we can achieve.

A Hidden History

Maybelle Blair, Shirley Burkovich and Thelma Eisen spent a Saturday at a special baseball clinic for young girls in Los Angeles. The three spent hours instructing the girls on the finer points of pitching, catching, hitting and base running.

Blair, Burkovich and Eisen aren't ordinary community volunteers but alumni of the All-American Girls Professional Baseball League during its heyday in the 1940s and 50s.

The League, which had largely been forgotten since it disbanded in 1954, inspired the popular 1992 movie, *A League of Their Own*. That helped re-ignite interest and increased awareness of women's professional baseball.

How much do you know about women's history? There is a wealth of available material. Make an effort to learn more about the way things really were.

Jesus said...'Mary!' ...Go to My brothers and say... I am ascending to My Father and Your Father'. (John 20:16,17)

Jesus who made Mary of Magdala Your Apostle to the Apostles, help us recognize the value of each person.

Choose Life

Dr. Ben Carson has been the director of pediatric neurosurgery at Johns Hopkins Children's Center since 1984. Not bad for a young man who found himself at the bottom of his class in fifth grade.

With guidance from what Carson refers to as his mother's firm hand, he says he realized he could change his circumstances by learning the information that would guarantee academic success.

"That would allow me to choose my own destiny," he wrote for *Parade* magazine. He committed himself, among other things, to reading the biographies of successful men and women. Along the way, Carson encountered negative people who tried to discourage him. He did not let them stand in his way.

His approach? "I chose to regard them simply as environmental hazards to be carefully swept aside," he says.

Never give in to discouragement.

The gifts He gave were...to equip the saints for the work of ministry, for building up the body of Christ. (Ephesians 4:11,12)

Let nothing come between me and my highest potential, Spirit of Power.

A Simple Hug

On the opening night of the Second Vatican Council, an occasion even more momentous than those who attended it likely realized, Pope John XXIII addressed a crowd of 50,000 that had assembled in St. Peter's Square.

"Go home and give your children a caress," he told them. "Tell them it is 'la carezza del Papa.' "

Kathy Coffey, author of *God Knows Parenting is a Wild Ride,* says that the comment spawned a new Italian tradition. Those who received a hug that night have passed it on to their own children. That one gesture, "la carezza di Papa Giovanni," continues to be passed from generation to generation.

How simple it is for us to start something good. A kind word, a thoughtful comment or an embrace of support have much more power than we realize. Too, more often than not, these actions are passed along, bringing new life to others as well.

Whoever does not receive the kingdom of God as a little child will never enter it. (Mark 10:15)

Jesus, may I share the love with which I have been blessed.

Voluntary Healing

At the Bowery Mission in New York City, residents and those who eat at its soup kitchen now enjoy free medical care because of volunteers like Dr. Brian Sumner and his wife, Leslee.

Leslee Sumner refers people at the mission to a store that offers free glasses and to a free program to quit smoking. She has also arranged for City Harvest, which collects surplus food from restaurants, caterers and hotels to teach a cooking and nutrition class to the homeless.

Jane Shin, a medical student, mentioned to Dr. Toni Sturm, that she was volunteering and together they arranged for 250 free flu and pneumonia shots. But Dr. Sumner notes the need for even more volunteer "nurses, nurse practitioners, physicians' assistants, social workers"–and for samples from drug companies.

Men and women in the healing professions have so much help and hope to offer those in trouble. So do we all.

**Hope deferred makes the heart sick.
(Proverbs 13:12)**

Fill us with hopeful helpfulness and optimism, Holy Spirit.

Are You In A Rut?

In a rut and want to get out? According to Nancy Evans, co-founder of a women's online network, you need to look inside and summon the courage to change and to stay motivated.

She also suggests:

1. Keep a list of everything good about your chosen change handy.
2. Write a letter explaining to yourself why you're making the change.
3. Practice your faith and pray to gain the peace to think straight, to try harder and to keep going.
4. Walk and meditate–somewhere scenic, if possible.
5. Find others who have had similar experiences so you will know what to expect and have supportive relationships, too.
6. Don't let things happen, make things happen.

To change is to grow, to be alive. Pray for the courage to change, grow, live.

Overcome evil with good. (Romans 12:21)

Holy God, inspire us to persevere in making positive changes.

Good Fortune

For D'Arcy Downs-Vollbracht good Fortune has four legs.

When Fortune was an unwanted yearling mare with a deformed hind foot, Downs-Vollbracht rescued her from being slaughtered for pet food.

Six years later, Fortune returned the favor. While Downs-Vollbracht was on crutches recuperating from a broken foot and tending her animals, a neighbor's three dogs attacked her goats, killing one. When she tried to intervene, one of the dogs turned on her.

That's when Fortune came to the rescue. "She kept lunging at the gate and finally broke out. It was totally intentional," said D'Arcy Downs-Vollbracht.

The 1300-pound yearling repelled the dogs, saved her owner and became locally famous. Fortune has become popular at community events, and has even helped raise thousands for charity.

Respect and value all creatures.

The horse is made ready for the day of battle, but the victory belongs to the Lord. (Proverbs 21:31)

Trinity, help us recognize the worth of all creatures.

Nancy's Stand

As the head waitress of a restaurant in the deep South of the 1950s, Nancy connected with her customers in any way she could. When a group of deaf students became regulars, for example, she studied sign language.

One day a group of soldiers stopped at the restaurant for a meal. The officer in charge asked where three black recruits could sit. In the South at the time, discrimination was institutionalized.

Nancy's response was simple. "They'll sit right here. ...If they're good enough to serve their country, they're certainly good enough to eat in our restaurant."

Several indignant customers left without paying their bills. Yet even more stood and applauded Nancy's decision. Decades later, one of the people there that day still remembers the head waitress's resoluteness as one of the most inspiring things she'd ever seen.

Compassion is a reward unto itself. Practice it.

Why do you pass judgment on your brother or sister? ...despise your brother or sister? For we will all stand before...God. (Romans 14:10)

Loving Father, help us to appreciate the humanity we share with all other people.

Garbage for the Kids

Men at the Kentucky State Penitentiary gather each morning to pick through the previous day's garbage. They remove pull-tabs from soft drink cans, then stomp and bag the cans for resale to the local recycling center.

"We're doing this for the kids, man," says prisoner Leo Spurling. One thousand pull-tabs pays for one hour of dialysis or chemotherapy for a child; 15,000 crushed cans bring in $200.

"I was as bad as a human being could get," Spurling recalls. "I had given up on life because I didn't know hope."

Then he and fellow inmate William Woolum talked about wanting to change and came up with the plan to recycle garbage to raise money for kids in need. Some prisoners also donate their own money, while others create craft items for sale.

"This program gives me hope," says Spurling.

All lives and all things have value—even lives and things seemingly thrown away. Where there is life, there is hope.

Do not be afraid; you are of more value than many sparrows. (Luke 12:7)

Bless my brokenness, Jesus, make me whole.

Unbroken Circle

In 1867, New York City firemen raised the money for what was then a cutting-edge hose carriage needed for the city of Columbia, South Carolina. The firemen sent it to Columbia as a peace offering in the aftermath of the Civil War.

City officials publicly thanked them, vowing to return the favor if New York City ever found itself in similar need.

Soon after September 11, 2001, Nancy Turner, a school principal in Columbia, started a campaign to buy a fire truck for New York City. Columbia's fire chief John Jansen, a New York native, told Turner of the historic implications. Students throughout the state, along with corporations and individual donors, raised more than $500,000 for the new fire truck.

Says Ms. Turner, "When your heart is in the right place anything is possible."

Do good with all your heart.

Love your enemies and pray for those who persecute you, so that you may be children of your Father in heaven. (Matthew 5:44)

Let us rejoice always in our opportunities to help our neighbors, wherever they are, Holy One.

One Family: The Human Family

"There's no difference between us, between Arab and Jew," said Abu Rumeileh. "God willing, there will be peace between us. That's the most important thing."

When 19-year-old Yoni Jesner, a Jewish student from Scotland died in a suicide bombing in Israel, his relatives donated his organs without knowing beforehand who would receive this great gift.

"They saved my daughter," said Abu Rumeileh. "Part of their son is living in my daughter. We are all one people."

The young Jesner's organ transplant now binds together two families. Yoni had planned to study medicine, according to his brother Ari who noted that Jewish and Arab doctors currently work side by side.

Ari Jesner says that 7-year-old Yasmin Rumeileh "suffered for years, and we're delighted to help. We believe it's a real sanctification of God's name to bring something out of this terrible conflict."

Let us pray and work for peace each and every day.

Hagar bore Abram a son; and Abram named his son... Ishmael. (Genesis 16:15)

Please grant us peace, Lord of all.

Sisterly Surprise

Tamara Rabi and Adriana Scott have a lot in common. They're both 5-foot-3-3/4 and in their early twenties. Both were born in Mexico and now live in New York. They also have the same birthday.

In fact, Tamara and Adriana are sisters. It's just that neither had any idea that the other existed.

The twins, adopted by different families while infants, found each other at college. Friends at Hofstra University were shocked by the uncanny resemblance between the two young women and put them in touch with each other. From there, the women pieced together the separate odysseys that led from their birth in Mexico to their reunion on Long Island.

Life can unfold in the most unexpected of ways. Take time to savor its surprises.

A tranquil mind gives life to the flesh. (Proverbs 14:30)

Spirit of Life, help us to appreciate all of life's twists.

Living the Golden Rule

"Do unto others as you would have them do unto you."

The familiar words of what has come to be known as the Golden Rule sound so simple, until you decide to live them.

Being consistent and persistent in doing unto others demands determination as well as good will. More over, we can only control our own attitudes and actions, not others'.

Still, many make a real effort, like the 93-year-old woman who had barely eked out a living as a farmer, then ended her days in a wheel chair. Her hard life didn't prevent her positive philosophy: "I always try to treat people just a little bit better than they treat me."

Then there's the businessman whose motto is "The Golden Rule applies, at all times, in all things, in all places."

Make the Golden Rule your own. You'll be in good company.

Do to others as you would have them do to you. (Matthew 7:12)

God, help me to love my neighbor as myself, for love of You.

A Philosophical Friend

Author Ronald Gross, who has delved deeply into the philosophies of Socrates, occasionally takes to the streets of New York City dressed like Socrates himself.

"I have been amazed by people's willingness to enter into meaningful dialogue," he says.

After years of study, Gross believes Socrates' chief values include authenticity, personal spirituality, friendship, and care of the soul. "I have been impressed by his relevance to our lives today," Gross observes.

One of Socrates' commitments was to grow with friends. Only in the moment of interaction, according to Gross, did Socrates believe that real understanding could occur.

Take time to visit with friends; they are more important than we realize. Watch for opportunities to raise the level of conversation to issues that everyone cares about.

Faithful friends are a sturdy shelter...beyond price...life-saving medicine. (Sirach 6:14,15,16)

Thank You, Holy Lord, for the way You speak to me through others.

Hope is the Little Thing

A few years ago cancer specialist Dr. Jerome Groopman had back surgery that failed. Walking more than a few blocks was impossible. Finally, he realized that his own hopelessness was making his situation worse. Dr. Groopman improved markedly.

Then a patient, a "very well-grounded, religious woman" taught Dr. Groopman that "you need to know everything that's blocking or threatening you. And then you see a path, or potential path." Even when this woman "no longer had choices or options about her body...she still had choices and options about her soul." She reconciled strained relationships and she sought the path to "a place where...her soul was at peace.

Those experiences convinced Dr. Groopman, who went on to write the book, *The Anatomy of Hope,* that the ancient Greeks were right: human beings cannot live without hope; without seeing "a path to the future."

Hope is the little thing that makes life livable.

Rejoice in hope. (Romans 12:12)

Sustain my hope, Holy Spirit.

Running on Prayer

Every day at 3:30 a.m. Mary Jo Copeland lets herself into St. Alphonsus church in Brooklyn Center, Minnesota, with her own key to begin a three-hour prayer regimen that includes power-walks while saying the rosary. "I wake up running to God," Copeland explains.

Growing up with an abusive father, Copeland found her salvation in prayer. Today she continues to draw strength from prayer and faith as she and her husband run Sharing and Caring Hands for the homeless and the working poor in downtown Minneapolis. They also help a home for children.

Sometimes called "America's Mother Teresa," Copeland encourages the children in her care to pray as well. And the boys and girls do pray, especially, they say, for Mary Jo Copeland.

Enliven your good works with the power of prayer.

**Do not grow weary when you pray.
(Sirach 7:10)**

From dawn's first light to the evening star, I offer You praise and give You thanks, my God.

A Lasting Tribute

Many of us commemorate the anniversary of the destruction of New York City's World Trade Center in different ways, public and private.

A nonprofit organization has "a simple idea," says David Paine, president of One Day's Pay: "Observe September 11 by doing something good for someone else." The inspiration was the passengers of United Airlines Flight 93, which crashed in a Pennsylvania field on September 11, 2001, during an attempt by the passengers to regain control of the plane from hijackers.

Jay Winuk, whose brother died at the World Trade Center, said: "We don't want to let go of that great sense of compassion that was so natural and so clearly demonstrated in so many ways by so many different kinds of people."

What better way to remember those who died? Let's all make a habit of compassion. The rewards are endless.

Moved with compassion, Jesus touched their eyes. Immediately they regained their sight and followed Him. (Matthew 20:34)

Father, make us instruments of merciful love.

The Worth of Work

If you've read the wonderful Christmas story, "The Other Wise Man," you know that Henry Van Dyke was the author. Besides being a writer, he was professor of English literature at Princeton University, U.S. minister to the Netherlands and a respected Presbyterian minister. Perhaps, it's not surprising that he wrote the following on labor:

"Let me but do my work from day to day,

In field or forest, at the desk or loom,

In roaring market-place, or tranquil room

Let me find it in my heart to say,

When vagrant wishes beckon me astray—

'This is my work—my blessing, not my doom—

Of all who live I am the one by whom

This work can best be done in my own way'."

Each of us can say the same: we have a job to do that belongs to no one else. Respect your work and give it your best.

Anna earned money at women's work. (Tobit 2:11)

Spirit of Wisdom, bless my work and my attitude toward it. And may my efforts be a blessing to others.

Got to Ramble On...

Audiences took to *School of Rock,* a movie comedy about a guitarist who poses as a substitute teacher and instructs his students how to appreciate the power of rock music.

Teacher David Wish runs a real life "School of Rock." The founder of Little Kids Rock, a non-profit organization that provides public schools with free instruments and music lessons, Wish began his program in 1996 when he borrowed instruments and began teaching his students music.

The program expanded when Wish recorded his students and sent CDs to local musicians known for philanthropic work. Soon, people like Santana and Bonnie Raitt became involved.

Little Kids Rock is now active in well over a hundred schools across the United States. "It's hundreds of teachers, thousands of kids, and it's free," Wish says.

Dedicating oneself to something he or she loves is just one way an individual can make a difference in the world. What can you do?

Let us consider how to provoke one another to love and good deeds. (Hebrews 10:24)

Lord, help us to utilize our full potential for good.

Yarr, Me Hearties!

It's likely you've heard of Captain Kidd, the infamous pirate who pillaged and marauded his way through the seas until he was caught and hanged. Yet that popular misconception overshadows the fact that Kidd was actually a pirate *hunter.*

As explained in Richard Zacks' *The Pirate Hunter,* Kidd was a respected captain hired to chase pirates and confiscate their pillage for his backers. Despite pressures to turn pirate, Kidd endured a mutiny rather than do so. When he learned of allegations that he had indeed pirated with his men, Kidd turned himself in, hoping to clear his name. Instead, forsaken by the lords who had backed his journey, he hanged.

So, it would seem, despite his gruesome end and centuries-old reputation, Kidd was an honorable man adrift in forces beyond his control. History can be wrong.

What else can you look at in a new light?

Some went down to the sea in ships, doing business on the mighty waters. (Psalm 107:23)

Trinity, help us to examine the world honestly.

Evelyn Trout: Trailblazer

When Evelyn Trout died at age 97, she was hailed as a pioneer in the field of aviation.

Her 2003 *New York Times* obituary noted Trout's achievements as a record-setting flier: the first woman to fly an aircraft all night; participant in the first so-called "Powder Puff Derby" (aka National Women's Air Derby); one of the first women to be a Los Angeles Police Department pilot.

Trout had a number of accomplishments in an era when women were constrained by society and the law. Despite obstacles, she followed her dreams.

We can't all become trailblazers, but we can break new ground in our personal lives. With confidence, courage and perseverance it is possible to continue learning and growing throughout life.

Wisdom is a fountain of life. (Proverbs 16:22)

Inspire us, Spirit of Life, to encourage young people to dream. Guide them as they pursue their aspirations.

Random Acts of Kindness

Where everyone is a stranger, it's easy to walk past a problem. But if instead you choose to help, you might be surprised at the ripple effect of random acts of kindness.

That's what happened to someone who told this story in *Bits & Pieces*.

"I met a friend after work for coffee. As we left the cafe, John and I saw two rush-hour commuters who clearly needed some help. A woman, who apparently had twisted her ankle, was leaning on the shoulder of another woman...the injured woman appeared to be in terrific pain."

Joining the first helper, John took the hurt woman's other arm for support; the writer called 911. "Another commuter stopped to ask if he could help. I said that an ambulance was on the way. 'I'll go down to the corner and flag them down,' said this newcomer."

Strangers together for a moment, doing the right thing.

I will pour out a spirit of compassion.
(Zechariah 12:10)

Lord, inspire me to an act of kindness today.

Ensuring Tolerance

Creation is proof of our Creator's delight in variety. There are Earth's infinite variety of mammals, fishes and birds. One example: consider the many kinds of dogs and cats.

Why then do we humans often reject diversity? Here are just a few suggestions for teaching tolerance:

- attend services at a variety of houses of worship
- go to an ethnic play or dance or listen to ethnic music
- take a civil rights history vacation
- pick a group, then see if any stereotypes about that group are reflected in your actions
- watch how you handle emotional issues with girls and boys
- push for paid maternity and paternity leaves
- be sure than anti-discrimination protections in your community extend to all people

If our Creator delights in diversity, shouldn't we, His creatures?

Judge your neighbor's feelings by your own. (Sirach 31:15)

Creator, forgive us our intolerance, our fear of "the other." Teach us to delight in all Your children as You do.

The Woman Who Put Up a Wall

Meg Falk was sitting in her Pentagon office on September 11, 2001, when she heard what she thought was a bomb blast.

As that day unfolded, the challenge to help hundreds of relatives desperate for information fell to Falk who heads the Defense Department's Office of Family Policy. Within 24 hours, she had set up a center at a local hotel for the victims' relatives. Falk and her team offered practical help, like helping to organize funerals and a table in the hotel ballroom where families could display pictures and mementos of their loved ones.

Today Meg Falk continues her mission of remembering the men and women who died at the Pentagon that day. She made an "American Heroes" wall: a bulletin board with the story and photograph of each victim. Each day she reads one, she says, "so I'll remember that these people were cherished members of families, of communities and of our country."

Remember the past. Work for the future.

I know that my Redeemer lives, and that at the last He will stand upon the earth; and after my skin has been thus destroyed, then in my flesh I shall see God. (Job 19:25-26)

Father, thank You for the gift of life eternal.

Best Recipe for Health-Urban Living?

"Urban sprawl," or the spreading out of populations beyond concentrated urban areas into suburbs, is a factor in obesity.

People who live in suburbs tend to drive everywhere and do not get exercise by walking. Fewer men and women are overweight or obese in neighborhoods where residents are more likely to walk to their destinations rather than drive.

Yet, no matter where a person lives, health and fitness can become part of one's daily routine. If you do live in a suburban or rural area, start out by taking just 10 minutes a day to walk around your neighborhood, a park or even a mall. Or, if your budget allows, join a gym.

Health is precious and should not be forfeited for the lack of exercise or the consumption of too much food. Look after yourself and your loved ones and try to keep your life balanced.

Better off poor, healthy, and fit than rich and afflicted in body. Health and fitness are better than any gold, and a robust body than countless riches. (Sirach 30:14-15)

I have a responsibility to take care of the body You gave me, Lord. Give me the discipline and perseverance to pursue a healthy lifestyle.

A Prayer for Today

Old forms of prayer can help us connect with our God. Here, for example, are excerpts from the "Southwell Litany:"

"O Lord, open our minds to see ourselves as Thou...or... others see us and we see others, and...to know our infirmities...

"From moral weakness...timidity; from hesitation; from fear of men and dread of responsibility, strengthen us with courage...

"From weakness of judgment...indecision... irresolution...

"Save us and help us, we humbly beseech Thee, O Lord.

"From weariness in continuing struggles; from despondency in failure and disappointment; from overburdened sense of unworthiness...raise us to a lively hope and trust in Thy presence and mercy.

"...give us knowledge of Thee, to see Thee in all Thy works, always to feel Thy presence near, to hear and know Thy call."

Pray.

Lord, teach us to pray. (Luke 11:1)

Encourage me to pray spontaneously at all times everywhere, Holy Spirit.

Persistence Starts Literacy Volunteers

Ruth Johnson Colvin never thought much about adult illiteracy until the 1960 census showed that thousands in her own city of Syracuse couldn't read. She decided to act.

Initially discouraged, she learned a valuable lesson. "It's a funny thing when you decide to give up," Ms. Colvin says. "You then let others help and it opens a door." Syracuse University professors helped her develop tutoring techniques.

Literacy Volunteers of America blossomed, reaching tens of thousands of students annually. In 2002, it joined with Laubach Literacy International to form ProLiteracy Worldwide, serving 350,000 adult learners in over 40 countries.

"Teaching literacy isn't just about giving people an important skill," says Ms. Colvin. "It's about breaking down racial, cultural and educational barriers. Bringing people together can change attitudes. It's like dropping a pebble in a pond. Once you do it, the ripples go on and on."

What ripples has your life created?

The wisdom of the scribe depends on the opportunity of leisure. (Sirach 38:24)

Jesus, bless all volunteers who give so generously of their time and talents.

Persuading, Gently, Forcefully

Are there times at work, at home or in a religious or social setting when you want to be persuasive? According to John Maxwell in his book, *Becoming a Person of Influence*, first, you need to be a person of integrity who is genuinely concerned for others and makes others feel good about themselves.

You also need to have faith in others and value them and their gifts. Tap into each person's passion; help others discover and move toward God's desire for them. And finally you need to let people know you don't take them for granted and that you want them to be their best.

Being influential means good will and hard work. Don't shirk it. Motivate others for good–their own, the world's.

The mind of the wise makes their speech judicious, and adds persuasiveness to their lips. (Proverbs 16:23)

God, inspire parents to motivate their children for good.

Let's Find a Cure

Popular columnist and humorist, Erma Bombeck died in 1996 from complication of PKD, or polycystic kidney disease. Though not well known, it's actually the most common life-threatening genetic disease in the United States, affecting more than 600,000 people.

PKD creates clusters of painful cysts on the kidneys. The kidneys then swell to football size, eventually shutting down in about 65 percent of patients.

Diagnosed at 19, Cecilia Maida thought she might die by age 30. But after learning she could possibly live longer, she decided to travel cross country, giving media interviews and telling others that PKD is "devastating entire families."

Her goal? To make PKD a household name; to get increased funding for research. "I'm not a religious fanatic, but I'm spiritual enough to see when a job has been put in front of me."

What job has been put in front of you?

Jesus went about...teaching...proclaiming the...kingdom, and curing every disease...When He saw the crowds, He had compassion for them. (Matthew 9:35,36)

Spirit of Life, heal the sick.

Kiddie Burnout?

Busy executives used to be considered almost synonymous with stress. But today, even children are overloaded and overbooked, with one extracurricular activity after another.

While developing interests and talents is important, loading up a youngster's day with activities can often do more harm than good. William Doherty, Ph.D., co-author of *Putting Family First*, says, "Too many children are tired and too many families are like ships passing in the night."

Doherty recommends scaling back children's schedules so they're more manageable. Most importantly, set aside family time to spend together talking and enjoying each other's company. That will calm kids and parents while fostering closeness.

Time really does fly—and it never comes back. Use it well.

He went down with them and came to Nazareth, and was obedient to them. (Luke 2:51)

Lord, help us find peace and quiet in our souls and in our families at the end of a hectic day.

Myths About Teenagers

"When my twin sons turned 12, I did what everybody told me to do, I waited. 'Just wait until they turn 13.' '...until they turn 14.'"

Writing in *Catholic Parent*, Deborah Hedestrom said she waited for the "promised teenage rebellion and it never came." What happened?

She believes that it's a mistake and a myth to think that: All teens will be a discipline problem; all teens and parents will not enjoy one another's company; all teens will use illegal drugs; all teens will be sexually promiscuous; all teens will stop practicing their faith.

Hedestrom advises parents not to panic over expected behavior and says, "It's normal for teens to tug on the reins of control." But adults should not abandon teens. Teens will test limits but this isn't necessarily a bad thing.

As with all aspects of life, do the very best you can, and leave the rest to God.

When He was twelve years old, they went up...for the festival. ...After three days they found Him...among the teachers...He said to them 'Why were you searching for Me'? (Luke 2:42,46,49)

Blessed Trinity, give parents the wisdom to guide young people to healthy and productive adulthood.

Dr. and Mrs. Samaritan

The person lies by the roadside, semi-comatose, half-dead. The family sits, waiting for someone to transport the sick one to the nearest medical facility several hours away.

And along come Dr. Scott Kellermann and his wife Carol. "We are amazed by their faith, because there is no public transport on these roads and vehicular traffic is rare," says the doctor.

As Episcopal missionaries in Uganda, he and his wife bring healing and hope to men, women and children with malaria and other illnesses. And they begin right there, on the side of the road.

One day, a 15-year-old boy approached the Kellermanns' small clinic, expressing his thanks for their saving his life. A week earlier, he had been a patient on the roadside. Now, he was returning to school. And, like many in Uganda, he was grateful to the Kellermanns.

Appreciate the help others give to you.

Were not ten made clean?...Was none of them found to return and give praise to God except this foreigner? (Luke 17:17)

Eternal God, lead me to do Your will, to serve Your people.

Mind Over Money Matters

Donna Meade-McMillan believes everyone needs and deserves an education. In fact, she originally came to the United States from her native Jamaica to attend college and later graduate school.

Now, Meade-McMillan uses her degree in communications to promote the Tri-County Scholarship Fund. It helps low-income New Jersey families pay their children's Catholic elementary and high school tuition. Since it was founded 20 years ago, 22,000 people have benefited from the more than $10 million distributed.

Tri-County is "not a hand-out," she says. "Parents...work together with us to give their kids a chance to move out of poverty."

Meade-McMillan continues, "I like my job. If you really like what you do, you do it with more passion."

Be passionate about your work—and about aiding the needy.

Give something to the poor. (John 13:29)

Teach me, Master, to do all You want of me.

Aim High and...Tall?

Does the name Daniel H. Burnham mean anything to you?

Burnham is one of the architects responsible for changing the world's skylines. His architectural vision helped pioneer the creation of the American skyscraper and develop New York's Flatiron Building and Washington, D.C.'s Union Station, as well as the 1893 World's Columbian Exposition in Chicago.

Burnham didn't plan for a future in architecture. He failed entrance exams to both Harvard and Yale, and attempted a political career, before finally returning to Chicago to apprentice as a draftsman. Soon after, he met his future architectural partner, John Wellborn Root.

Burnham is best known for the *Plan of Chicago* developed in 1909. This proposed plan set a standard for urban design. "Make no little plans," Burnham said. "They have no magic to stir men's blood...Make big plans, aim high in hope and work."

Never give up on building your dreams.

The plans of the diligent lead surely to abundance. (Proverbs 21:5)

Help me find the drive to achieve my dreams, Savior.

Weekends–and God

Popular wisdom: *All* people with weekend homes and those who go away for weekends omit God from their plans. Fact: For many, a weekend away is for playing and napping–and God.

Pierre Schoenheimer likes sitting in the sanctuary of the Jewish Center of the Hamptons. "It seems more spiritual, closer to nature and closer to God."

At the Squaw Valley Chapel, Pastor Stephen Hamilton says "we embrace the sacred of the environment" as he leads worshipers out to see wildflowers after services.

Julie FitzPatrick finds the informality of country worship "not a bad thing" after the formality of the work week.

Marilise Flusser says that "if a practice works…during the week, why give it up when you're relaxing?"

Another says "The church in the country is smaller and more intimate. It makes it easier to be more connected."

Connect with God wherever you are.

When He came to Nazareth, where He had been brought up, He went to the synagogue on the Sabbath day, as was His custom. (Luke 4:16)

Holy God, help us to include You in our weekends.

A Body Destroyed, a Faith Restored

Jim McLaren is no stranger to setbacks. At age 22, McLaren was hit by a bus while riding his motorcycle, and his left leg was amputated. Eight years later, he was hit by a van while competing in a triathlon. This time, McLaren awakened a paraplegic.

Although he had recovered well after the first accident, McLaren started to lose hope after the second accident destroyed his mobility. He secretly turned to cocaine to help numb the pain. After months of drug abuse, McLaren searched for a reason behind his suffering. He found comfort in the biblical story of Job. McLaren says, "I needed these accidents to bring me...to a place where I could find...peace."

Today, he is drug-free and pursuing a doctorate degree.

Even seemingly insurmountable obstacles can be overcome with faith.

Naked I came from my mother's womb, and naked shall I return there; the Lord gave, and the Lord has taken away; blessed be the name of the Lord. (Job 1:21)

Almighty One, help me understand the mystery of suffering in my own life and in others'.

If We Genuinely Want Healthy Families...

To get new mothers out of the house and into adult company for a few unstructured hours once a month, Shara Frederick organized Tots and Tonic.

Tea and coffee are as popular as wine or beer; sofas and organic snacks, a draw at the restaurants where they meet. One of the mothers, Pamela Foster, found it good to be able to talk with adults on topics other than babies and mothering if she wanted to.

And by the way, no one objected to a crying baby–at one time or other all the babies were crying!

If we want healthy families we need healthy mothers. That means quality family policies at work, including health care programs; and supportive and recreational programs for at-home mothers and their children.

Offer what practical help you can to young parents.

The Lord...confirms a mother's right over her children. (Sirach 3:2)

Jesus, since families are the foundation of society, remind us to be genuinely supportive of parents and children.

Harvesting Hope

When St. Frances de Sales parish in Lake Zurich, Illinois, was ready to mark its 50th anniversary, there were many suggestions for the celebration.

The winning idea: Parishioners would plant a farm.

Patches of potatoes, onions, zucchini, Swiss chard, carrots, corn, dill and more dot the 10-acre field. Most of the food is donated to local soup kitchens and food pantries. The rest of the harvest is sold on Sunday mornings to raise money for expenses, including seeds. Surplus funds are given to hunger-related charities.

Says George Koll, pastoral associate at the parish, "people are using it to teach their kids about the growing cycle and about social justice. Parishioners are working shoulder-to-shoulder. It is a real faith sharing."

It looks as though the greatest crops harvested at this farm are hope and love.

Praise Him for His mighty deeds; praise Him according to His surpassing greatness!...Let everything that breathes praise the Lord! (Psalm 150:2,6)

May our lives and actions praise You, Beloved Father. May we give You thanks for Your many gifts to us.

A True Pioneer

By the time Althea Gibson died in 2003, a black woman playing tennis was no longer unusual.

But when Gibson emerged into the world of tennis in the 1950s, she was the first black player to compete in the United States nationals. She went on to win 56 tournaments, including five Grand Slam singles titles.

Historical context helps bring new life to the impact individuals have made on our society. Much of what is now commonplace was once revolutionary. Yet no revolution, especially one for equality before the law and justice in every situation is fixed, secure for all time.

The revolution begun in 1776 needs to be on-going. Do your part, not only for the people of today, but those of tomorrow.

Proclaim liberty throughout the land to all its inhabitants. (Leviticus 25:10)

Author of our Liberties, may I be inspired by previous generations' struggles for liberty, justice and equality for all. May I carry on their struggles in these perilous times.

Paint It Black

Many people saw a recent movie about the brave drillers who plant a nuclear bomb in an asteroid on a collision course with Earth in order to save our planet. Scientists who study asteroids, though, have quite a different take on how to deal with such a scenario.

A nuclear detonation on or near an asteroid set to strike Earth would, in actuality, fragment the space rock and create a more widespread threat. In one of the more subtle alternatives, the asteroid would be painted black. The black coating would alter the asteroid's course by absorbing the sun's heat and causing a higher rate of thermal photon transmission on the asteroid's surface. Essentially, the asteroid would be moved from its path one tiny particle at a time.

Sometimes the subtlest solutions to a problem are the most powerful. Consider that before reacting to any situation.

Decide with equity for the meek. (Isaiah 11:4)

Holy Spirit, help us to see all the alternatives before us.

Changing for the Better

Would you like to change your life? Find more joy and serenity?

Here are suggestions from Salley Shannon writing in *Woman's Day* magazine:

- Be attentive to your physical health. Care for yourself. Rest. Eat nutritiously. Rest some more.
- See the inner person you would like to be. Pray daily. Choose virtue: be just, truthful, fair, kind.
- Turn away from anger and blame through forgiveness. By "changing your mental channel," you can keep bad memories from controlling you.
- Make the life **you** enjoy. Discover what you love and do as much as you can, as often as you can.
- Scrap perfectionism. You need neither to prove you are worthy nor to please anyone.

You were made for joy and serenity. Embrace them.

I came that they may have life, and have it abundantly. (John 10:10)

Abide with me, Good Shepherd.

Borders? What Borders?

They are Jews, they are Quakers and other Christians and they are Muslims. A grassroots group formed in the aftermath of the September 11 terrorist attacks and called itself Women Transcending Borders. The topics they discuss range from death and dying to the way the F.B.I. handled the arrests of three local men.

Betsy Wiggins, one of the two founders of the group, says listening and learning are key. Their discussions have led to action, and they recently raised nearly $8000 to support two schools in Pakistan. Given that the annual budget for each school is $1,500, the project made a huge impact.

"We're a little microcosm of Syracuse, New York, of the United States, of the world," says Wiggins. "If we can't talk honestly in our own little group, if we can't work together to make a difference, what hope is there?"

There is hope. Keep talking and working for peace.

Great peace have those who love Your love. (Psalm 119:165)

Spirit of Truth, give us the courage to reach out to people of other nations, as we seek peace-filled justice for all.

A Loan to Grow

Guadalupe Castillo Ureña, widowed at 31, scraping by on $2 a day or less, found herself alone with her five children in her native Mexico.

Then an organization named Finca offered her the opportunity to borrow money to start her own business.

Ureña took the chance, borrowing $250 to buy the clay and firewood needed to make hundreds of clay pots. After selling them and repaying the loan, she had money left to feed her children and pay their school fees. "It's something," Ureña said. "An opportunity."

Mary O'Keefe, who helped start Finca's operations in Mexico a decade ago, said the loan program comes with "the realization that poor people are deserving of financial services."

Everyone needs a helping hand at some time in life. Do what you can to assist your neighbors, wherever and whoever they are.

The merciful lend to their neighbors; by holding out a helping hand they keep the commandments. (Sirach 29:1)

Almighty and Eternal God, You are the strength, the refuge, the hope of Your people.

No Wrong Number

Cheryl and Mike Tabak of South Carolina can show us what it means to be good neighbors–and good listeners. When their phone number was mistakenly listed as an alternative for the local electric company, they took the occasional errant calls in stride, giving people the correct number.

Then an ice storm knocked out the electricity to two million customers. Their phone rang constantly for a week.

But the Tabaks didn't take it off the hook. Instead, they continued to exhibit the good humor and grace they had shown before–2600 times! They offered distraught customers advice, kindness and in one case groceries. Why?

In 1989 their home had been destroyed by Hurricane Hugo. Cheryl says, "I know what it's like to live through a bad storm. A lot of people just need a sympathetic ear."

Being a good listener is a gift. Do you know someone with whom you can share it?

Listen carefully. (Isaiah 55:2)

Make me a patient and attentive listener, Jesus.

Choosing Forgiveness, Choosing Life

Bill Pelke's grandmother had been murdered by four teenage girls. One, Paula Cooper, was on death row.

Pelke decided to forgive her. He prayed for love and compassion. The thought of her execution horrified him.

They met. Pelke wrote articles, collected signatures on a petition and talked about forgiveness. In time, Cooper was removed from death row.

Next, Pelke and others in a similar situation began Murder Victims' Families for Reconciliation and speaking tours called 'Journey of Hope.' These offer "hope in the power of forgiveness and hope in the possibility of a world without violence."

A woman whose pregnant sister and brother-in-law had been murdered said, "executing a murderer (does) not make the victim's family feel better, but only adds to the violence and killing."

Choose life and forgiveness personally, locally, internationally. Do not add to the violence and killing.

Be at peace with one another. (Mark 9:50)

Holy Spirit, give us the courage to choose forgiveness over revenge; peace over war; life over death.

America's Favorite Underdog

Legendary horse trainer Tom Smith is best known for turning a small and neglected thoroughbred into a national icon.

Seabiscuit captured the collective imagination of Americans looking to escape from Depression-era hardship. Though rarely the favorite, in races he won and even in those he lost "by a nose," people saw this underdog as their champion.

But it wasn't always that way. When Smith first encountered Seabiscuit in 1936, he was undernourished, refusing to eat and nervous. He charged at anyone who came near him.

So how did Tom Smith turn Seabiscuit around? "Horses stay the same from the day they are born until the day they die...They are only changed by the way people treat them," he said.

Our actions have more of an effect on others than we can possibly imagine. Treat all residents of God's earth with respect and loving care.

Like clay in the hand of the potter...so all are in the hand of their Maker. (Sirach 33:13)

Father, you have made us stewards of Your creatures. Enable us to respect and nurture them; delight in them, too.

Bless This House—and Here's How

Home is the place where we rest and celebrate; where love and comfort are given and received. It's a natural place to create holy ground. How to express the sacredness of our homes? With such symbols as these:

Mezuzahs are parchment scrolls inscribed with Deuteronomy 6:4-9 and 11:13-21, rolled up in a decorative container and nailed to the right doorposts of Jewish homes, as a sign of faith and a reminder of God's abiding presence.

In Christian homes, a crucifix or cross affixed to a wall, is a sign of faith in Jesus as our Redeemer, and a reminder that even in life's darkest times we are never alone.

Adding objects that are personally meaningful, such as beautiful plants, sweet-scented candles, or a wind chime can play a spiritual role.

Greater than all these signs of the sacred is the love for one another which permeates a home and mirrors God's love for us.

Love one another with mutual affection; outdo one another in showing honor. (Romans 12:10)

Almighty God, may we feel Your strength and Your love.

Saved by the Kindness of a Stranger

Things looked grim for Mark Zelermyer's wife. Her kidney disease, under control with medication for over 20 years, had begun to worsen. All potential kidney donors among family and friends had been tested and eliminated.

Then, one evening, as Zelermyer rode home on the train with Carolyn Hodges, a friend from work, he told her the whole story. The next day Hodges approached Zelermyer at work. She and her husband had talked it over and were willing to be tested as potential matches. Carolyn was eliminated, but her husband, John, whom the Zelermyers barely knew, was the donor of choice.

The transplant operation was a success. When questioned about his decision to help a virtual stranger, John Hodges said he felt this was his way to actively make the world a better place.

No matter what the degree, helping others always means an investment of self done with love.

This is My commandment, that you love one another as I have loved you. (John 15:12)

Merciful Savior, thank You for providing for my every need. May I express my gratitude through loving generosity to others.

Who Packed Your Parachute?

Charles Plumb, a U.S. Navy jet pilot, ejected and parachuted from his plane when it was shot down over Vietnam. Surviving the ordeal of six years in a Communist Vietnamese prison, he lectures today on lessons learned from the experience.

One day, Plumb and his wife were sitting in a restaurant when a man approached them. "You're Plumb!" he said. "You flew jet fighters in Vietnam and were shot down. I packed your parachute."

Plumb wondered how many times he had seen that man and not even said hello.

Now when Plumb speaks on his experiences, he asks, "Who's packing your parachute?" He encourages others to find the people in their lives who offer them the physical, mental and emotional help that lifts them up and carries them through difficult times. And he suggests that people recognize and give thanks for them and to them.

Raphael...said to them, "Bless God and acknowledge Him in the presence of the living for the good things He has done for you. (Tobit 12:6)

Father, send Your angels to be with me.

Helping Youngsters Bridge Differences

When *Women's Day* magazine established its first annual awards ceremony to honor inspiring women, one recipient was thirty-one-year-old Lisa Navarra.

As an associate director for youth and children's ministries at St. John's Episcopal Church in McLean, Virginia, she tries to bring together low-income teens from Washington, D.C. with the more affluent young people from her town.

"When kids from D.C. come into the program, they think they're completely different from the kids who live in McLean, and vice versa," noted Navarra. But once they're "on the basketball court or play volleyball together," notes Navarra, "they realize their similarities outweigh their differences and that their differences can help them broaden each other's worlds."

It's so easy to think we know all there is about people based on their background, their looks or where they are from. So often we would be wrong. Open your mind and heart to all.

Pay...respect to whom respect is due, honor to whom honor is due.(Romans 13: 7)

Inspire us, Holy Spirit, to better understand the world and the wisdom of those around us.

A Dog's Life—in Pictures

Just about everyone, it seems, has seen or joked about those pictures showing cigar-smoking dogs playing poker, imitating very serious human gamblers.

Do we know the artist of these paintings? Most would be hard pressed to identify Cassius Marcellus Coolidge as the painter. It was he who thought up the idea of painting dogs in a human setting. He even titled one "A Friend in Need," rather than "Dogs Playing Poker," the most commonly used title.

While some consider Coolidge's paintings the subject of derision or mild amusement, others see a deep symbolism and irony in his work. A Coolidge original sold for $74,000 at a large art auction, hardly the cost of a frivolous piece of art.

What one values, another considers useless, and vice versa. Sometimes we find treasures in what others discard. It's all part of what makes us one-of-a-kind.

We have this treasure in clay jars, so that it may be made clear that this extraordinary power belongs to God and does not come from us. (2 Corinthians 4:7)

Thank You for my originality and idiosyncrasies, Father, for these are is what make me unique.

A Dollar a Dinner

In Brampton, a Toronto, Ontario suburb, one popular restaurant serves over 54,000 meals a year at a dollar a meal. Most of its customers are homeless, downtrodden, or in need of help.

In 1990, Cecil Peters and his daughter saw someone rummaging through garbage for food. Peters decided to appeal to his fellow Knights of Columbus to fight hunger in their town.

The result was The Knights Table restaurant. Local markets, farmers and restaurant chains donate food; volunteers come from corporations and public and private schools; and money arrives from foundations and individuals.

In this restaurant, dignity, respect and friendship come with the meal. Says Brian, "They go out of their way here...It's more like going home to dinner when we were kids."

Offer friendship as well as charity to those less fortunate than you.

Is not this the fast that I choose: to loose the bonds of injustice...to let the oppressed go free...to share your bread with the hungry. (Isaiah 58:6,7)

Merciful Savior, help me see You in the hungry and homeless.

To Ellis Island–and Home

What do Irving Berlin, Bob Hope, and Claudette Colbert have in common with Father Edward Flanagan, Knute Rockne and the von Trapp family? Ellis Island.

Between 1892 and 1954 12 million immigrants passed through Ellis Island in New York Harbor. After traveling for weeks, generally in steerage, men women and children in search of a better future, took their first steps in their new home.

They came from Italy, Russia, Ireland and dozens of others countries, with everything they had, from clothing to pots and pans. After medical exams, those who failed were deported. But the vast majority were in America to stay, to become citizens and to make their mark in a land that promised the one thing most would otherwise never have had: the gift of opportunity.

And just like those who came here before and since, they gave to their new home the gift of themselves.

You and the alien who resides with you shall have the same law and the same ordinance. (Numbers 15:16)

Blessed Lord, thank You for Your many gracious gifts. Help us use them well for ourselves and for our neighbors.

Just Part of the Job

Businessman Dave Zapatka believes "there is no higher calling than serving other people."

As a young man working in a fast-food restaurant, one of Zapatka's regular customers gave him a copy of Khalil Gibran's book *The Prophet.* He was struck by the sentence: "It is well to give when asked, but it is better to give unasked, through understanding."

Zapatka who founded a Missouri-based cleaning company with hundreds of employees, noticed that many people were unable to read the job application. He devised his own test: read the label on a bottle of cleaning fluid.

If applicants couldn't do it, but Zapatka wanted to hire them, they had to agree to attend free weekly tutoring sessions. Those who stuck it out confirmed his belief that reading makes people better employees and more productive members of society.

We can do so much for others, asked or unasked.

When you give alms, do not let your left hand know what your right hand is doing. (Matthew 6:4)

Holy Spirit, inspire us to find ways to serve others.

Java for a Just Price

For those of you who long for the days when a cup of coffee cost a reasonable price, you're not alone. While the cost of a cup of coffee has skyrocketed, most of that money never makes it to the growers of those coffee beans.

Rink Dickinson and Jonathan Rosenthal had an idea that grew into an extraordinary business model: purchase coffee beans directly from farming cooperatives, eliminate middlemen, and put more money into growers' hands, while keeping per-cup costs reasonable. Their efforts have directly benefited growers in Guatemala, Colombia and Nicaragua where profits are essential to land ownership and survival. Consumers are behind this success.

They say, "Consumers have phenomenal power in this society and really have just barely begun to use it."

You do have the power to effect change. And it can mean all the difference in the world to someone in need.

Seek good and not evil. (Amos 5:14)

I will work harder to take my rights and privileges as a citizen more seriously, Lord.

Vocations for All

The new hot topic on college campuses has little to do with pop culture or politics. What's the buzz? Vocations.

Notre Dame junior Kristy Hernandez believes that "just because I will have an office job in corporate America does not mean I cannot have a vocation." Instead of limiting the idea of vocation to vowed religious life, ordained ministry or service with groups such as the Peace Corps, students like Kristy Hernandez are embracing the notion of vocation as a part of daily living.

Stephen Camilleri, director of the Notre Dame Vocation Initiative said, "Ultimately, we want students and faculty to look at how they are called and how they can use their gifts to change the world."

We can all ask these question of ourselves: What is my vocation? And within that call how can I use my gifts for the greater good of all?

To each is given the manifestation of the Spirit for the common good. (1 Corinthians 12:7)

Spirit of Counsel, may we employ the many talents with which You have blessed us for the benefit of all.

Making Public Housing Homey

To many people, public housing is dismal, depressing, even dangerous.

David J. Burney sees differently. While acknowledging that most public housing is inadequately designed, Burney believes "there are still things you can do about it." And because he's an architect and Director of Design and Capital Improvement for the New York City Housing Authority he can sometimes bring his vision to fruition.

In fact, a Sloan Public Service Award noted that "he has changed many places from an eyesore to something that residents can be proud of. It's a major transformation in public housing."

When Burney spruces up public housing he also improves thousands of lives. Says one resident: "Every day, I have the good fortune of waking up and looking out the window at a garden. I can go outside."

Every job offers opportunities to do good.

The necessities of life are water, bread, and clothing, and also a house to assure privacy. (Sirach 29:21)

Creator, inspire the labors of architects and builders.

Frayed Ends of Sanity, Recovered

James Hetfield prided himself on being the man in charge.

As co-founder of the heavy metal band Metallica, Hetfield had built a career on seeming tougher than most. A notorious control freak, he insisted on co-writing all of the band's songs and even tried to dictate what side projects band members could be involved in. That changed, however, when his control issues drove bassist Jason Newsted to quit after 14 years with the band.

"Jason leaving was a catalyst," according to Hetfield. It caused self-examination that eventually led Hetfield to realize he was "broken and dragging the bottom." Rather than risk losing his life and family, he checked into rehab for alcohol problems he had previously been unwilling to admit.

"I refer to rehab as college for my soul," he says. Ultimately, Hetfield learned that he was "human...I could ask for help."

We all need help sometimes. Allow yourself to ask for it.

O my Lord, You only are our king; help me, who am alone and have no helper but You. (Add. Esther 14:3)

Lord, help us to recognize when we need help and to be humble enough to ask for it.

Current – but Old-fashioned – Technologies

Have all older technologies have been swept away? Here are just few of the many that remain in use.

Analog watches. The kind with a dial and hands that sweep round the dial to mark the time. Excruciatingly expensive models are now adult trophies.

Dot-matrix printers. Need to print reams of data speedily, reliably, cheaply? Dot-Matrix printers, now called "impact printers," can print over 500,000 pages a month at less than 1/5¢ per page.

Typewriters both electric and manual. They are unaffected by viruses, hard drive failure and corrupted software. Some prefer simplicity and do not want to learn computers.

Fax machines. Real estate firms and lawyers run on them because they remain the fastest way to send on-paper images, documents and marked-up text.

Neither what's new nor what's old are necessarily bad. Each has its niche. Treasure both.

How much more valuable is a human being. (Matthew 12:12)

Holy Spirit, enlighten us.

Order in the Court

D.J. Davis attended law school for just one reason: to offer low income families good legal representation.

When Davis attended college in Nashville, becoming a lawyer wasn't her primary goal until she met a family with legal problems which lacked money to hire a lawyer. She said, "It was painful to see the girls and their mother endure such a traumatic experience."

Davis opened the non-profit Jericho Community Law Office in 2001 and has provided inexpensive legal aid at no more than $500 per case. Local churches and ministries are the financial backbone of the office. Davis's next goal: to improve Tennessee's foster care system.

D. J. Davis says that she comes to people "with the servant-like attitude Jesus demonstrated."

Show your faith through your actions, your service.

Faith by itself, if it has no works, is dead. (James 2:17)

May we follow Your example of loving service, Jesus.

Where Art Thou?

Walter Persegati, former secretary and treasurer of the Vatican Monuments, Museums, and Galleries, has no doubt about the highlight of his career. In fact, he calls the fourteen years he spent overseeing the cleaning and restoration of Michelangelo's murals in the Vatican's Sistine Chapel the high point of his life.

Today, in lectures explaining the process to audiences around the world, his enthusiasm is still tangible. He speaks of his crew being dwarfed by the artwork once they climbed the scaffolding and says there is no way to express the feelings of being surrounded by the art.

Persegati believes those visiting the Sistine Chapel today are seeing it through Michelangelo's eyes. "You can see what Michelangelo wanted to tell us," he enthuses.

He also says the project allowed him to go beyond discovering the artist and into a spiritual renewal.

Where in your daily life do your find God?

Seek the Lord and His strength; seek His presence continually. (Psalm 105:4)

Help us to find You, God, in our daily responsibilities.

Clothes Make the Worker

"If you are unemployed and need an outfit clean for a interview, we will clean it for free," read a sign in the window of Carlos Vasquez's Manhattan dry cleaners shop.

Mr. Vasquez's upper East side Manhattan area suffered the most casualties of any one community in the destruction of New York City's World Trade Center–44 neighbors.

The loss of local financial and advertising positions since then has cost the neighborhood a disproportionate number of jobs.

For a while five or six people came in each month to have interview clothes cleaned; lately, two or three. Mr. Vasquez asks to see an unemployment check stub. But he will also take the customer's word.

Carlos Vasquez is doing what he can to help a wounded neighborhood.

What are you doing to help those bruised by life?

The measure you give will be the measure you get back. (Luke 6:38)

Holy Spirit, inspire and strengthen us to help those afflicted by life's hardships.

A Touch of Humor

For writer Louise Erdrich, who is of German, French and Ojibwe heritage, humor plays a role in her stories and her life. She set out to learn Ojibwemowin, the language of her mother's people, so she could understand the jokes.

"Words are constantly in a state of flux and invention, and a fluent speaker can inject humor into any subject or situation with a vowel, or a mere crumb of a verb reference," said Erdrich. "As for humor in my fiction...it's impossible to write about...life without humor–that's how people maintain sanity."

Touches of humor shine through even the darkest moments in the world of Erdrich's fictional characters.

Humor surrounds us in the real world, too. Take a peek around and learn to laugh a little. Life is too short to ignore a good joke in any language.

A person's....hearty laughter...show(s) what he is. (Sirach 19:30)

May we see and enjoy the humor in life, Heavenly Father.

Flying Through Barriers

At the tender age of 19, Roscoe Brown resigned from the Civilian Military Training Corps to become a member of the now-famed Tuskegee Airmen. These men were the first all-black military squadron and the most successful bomber-escort company in World War II.

Though the Tuskegee Airmen faced many roadblocks on their journey to respect and recognition, breaking through racism was crucial not only for themselves but for generations to come. "Knowing that everything you did was being examined–that was the most difficult thing," said Brown. "(But it's) the most significant thing in my life, because we helped to change the country."

For Roscoe Brown, the security of a lieutenant's commission in a civilian unit couldn't compare to the possibility of securing a better future for all.

Taking chances is never easy and the road is often long and hard, but the rewards are endless.

Stand firm in your faith. (1 Corinthians 16:13)

You are always with us, O Lord, picking us up whenever we fall and giving us the courage to stand. Thank You.

Eat Your Peas

Rick Beyer despised peas. Luckily, he was never forced to eat them—until one fateful day when he was eight.

Rick, his mother and his grandmother were eating in a restaurant when his grandmother insisted he eat his peas. A battle of wills began when Rick's mother contradicted her. His grandmother finally played her trump card when she made Rick an offer: "I'll pay you five dollars if you eat those peas."

Rick greedily ate his peas and received his payment. He realized the true price of those peas, however, a few weeks later when Rick's mother served him a steaming pile of the vegetables. When Rick refused them, his mother played *her* trump card: "You ate them for money. You can eat them for love." Rick was then forced to eat his peas whenever they were served.

Immediate rewards can be enticing, but may also carry unforeseen consequences. Give thought to your actions.

Commit your work to the Lord, and your plans will be established. (Proverbs 16:3)

Savior, help us to recognize that all of our actions bear meaning.

Greater than Fear

"The biggest straitjacket is all the prejudices that we carry around, and all the fears," says renowned Chilean writer Isabel Allende. "But what if we just surrender to the fear? There are things greater than fear....we can overcome even absolute terror, and we do."

Straitjacket is a good word to describe the way prejudices squeeze and narrow the mind; fears, the soul. It takes courage to break free of the constraints that lock us within ourselves, and not our best selves, at that.

Here's what another great writer had to say about this necessary quality. According to Samuel Clemens, also known as Mark Twain, "Courage is resistance to fear, mastery of fear–not absence of fear."

We humans have always been pretty good at overcoming what holds us back. We just have to give ourselves a chance.

Be courageous and valiant. (1 Kings 2:2)

Spirit of Courage, let me rely on Your strength when I have none of my own.

Where's the Poet?

Romantic poet John Keats didn't start off as a great poet. In fact, he didn't start off as a poet at all. In 1811, Keats was apprenticed to a surgeon and five years later completed his professional training. Later he dedicated himself to his poetry.

Some have called Keats' decision to commit himself to poetry a courageous one, but contemporary critics regarded him as a "lower-class vulgarian, with no right to aspire to poetry." His first collection, *Poems,* published in 1817, was a failure, but Keats kept writing.

His determination, hard work and belief in himself paid off in the end. John Keats died in 1821 at the age of 26, having received some critical recognition for his final work. Today, he is recognized as one of the premier poets of English Romanticism.

Never give up on your dreams, and always believe in yourself and others.

Prosper the work of our hands! (Psalm 90:17)

Father, bless us with determination and give us the strength to believe in ourselves when times appear their darkest.

Dissecting the Diorama

One would wonder why, in the days of interactive video-based displays and downloadable remote web casts, the American Museum of Natural History would spend millions to update and restore the dioramas in its 70-year old Hall of Ocean Life.

It turns out those stodgy old dioramas still have some value. They serve as "libraries of our species," as one museum vice-president put it, bringing painstakingly detailed, and sometimes extinct, ecosystems directly to viewers. For instance, the Bahamian Coral Reef Group diorama required multiple expeditions to the real reefs and the transport of over 40 tons of coral. The diorama could not be recreated now, as the reefs have been ecologically degraded in the intervening years.

It's easy to be impressed by new technology and innovation, but we shouldn't forget the value of what we already have.

No one after drinking old wine desires new wine, but says, 'The old is good'." (Luke 5:39)

Lord, help us to appreciate all we have, new and old.

From Setback to Comeback

"Setbacks make great opportunities for comebacks," says San Jose State Coach Fitz Hill. The comment was made in reference to a player who served as tremendous inspiration for both Hill and the team he coaches.

It all started in October of 2000 when Neil Parry broke his leg during a game against the University of Texas at El Paso. Within nine days, an infection necessitated the amputation of his leg below the knee. Hours after the operation, Parry told his family he would one day play football again.

No one stood in the way of this young man's determination, and 25 operations, a prosthetic leg, and three years later, Parry suited up and joined the Spartans in their game against Nevada.

"I didn't even think about missing my leg," he later told a reporter. "I just thought about what I had to do."

Think about what's important to you–and give it all you've got.

Hope does not disappoint us. (Romans 5:5)

When little things discourage me, Jesus, help me to accept myself as I am and to cling to You.

One Part Smile, One Part Tears

Over a decade ago, radio disc jockey Scott Shannon and the rest of his "Big Show" team did their first broadcast at Blythedale Children's Hospital in Valhalla, New York.

Seeing the tiny gurneys and wheelchairs hit home for the radio gang. "You realize that they're for all these children who don't deserve to be in this situation, but who are," Shannon says.

Since then, the show's finale at Blythedale has become an annual event with big name musicians putting on a concert for the kids. The Big Show also sponsors an auction and fund raiser for the hospital.

"For most people, life isn't all laughter and it isn't all tears," Shannon says. "We entertain people...but we also have a responsibility. ...This is our most important show of the year."

One part smile, one part tears, all parts love. Show someone you care today and every day.

(Jesus) took the child's father and mother and those who were with Him, and went in where the child was. He took her by the hand and said to her, "Talitha cum." ...immediately the girl got up. (Mark 5:40-41,42)

Child of Nazareth, watch over all children.

Courage Like No Other

Beatings, kidnapping, robbery and death threats were all in a day's work to Annalena Tonelli, during her 33-year career.

Tonelli was not a soldier or a police officer, as one might surmise. A lawyer as well as a medical doctor she devoted her life to eradicating disease in Northwest Somalia.

Political strife, harsh climate, desert terrain and poverty made conditions extremely dangerous. Yet, Dr. Tonelli was unfazed, loved every aspect of her work and relied on no organizations or institutions for support—just family and friends.

Annalena Tonelli was murdered in October, 2003 at the entrance to her tuberculosis hospital in Borama, Northwest Somalia. She was sixty years old.

Doctor Tonelli pursued her mission without hesitation—and that enabled her to endure the unimaginable.

Is your work furthering your unique mission on earth?

Is there no balm in Gilead? Is there no physician there? Why then has the health of my poor people not been restored? (Jeremiah 8:22)

God, give me the courage to live the life I was born to live.

Bully for You!

An elementary school in a small city in northwest Pennsylvania defines "bullying as any word, look, sign, or act that inflicts or threatens to inflict physical or emotional injury or discomfort upon another person's body, feelings, or possessions."

That's a stringent definition when you think about it. Giving someone a look that even threatens to inflict discomfort upon his or her feelings falls under this definition. And yet we all indulge in this behavior more frequently than we'd like to admit.

And kids pick up on our actions much more easily than our words. So until we stop bullying them and each other, it's unlikely we'll see real improvement in the way they treat each other.

But it's worth the effort in school and at home. Do your part to create a peaceful, respectful environment.

A harvest of righteousness is sown in peace for those who make peace. (James 3:18)

Remind me, Creator, that my conduct influences my children's conduct.

Less Stress, More Peace

Many people seem to have forgotten *how* to relax and find themselves filling otherwise peaceful moments with more stress.

Here are some tips on decompressing when stress hits:

- On a scale of one to ten, with ten being a disaster, how upset are you? With this momentary examination, problems are put into a more realistic and less threatening perspective.
- Be ready for difficulties. You'll be better able to avert them, and less bothered when they occur. Stress has its roots in unrealistic expectations, so accept mishaps as part of any routine.
- Choose your own relaxing image. Whenever your stress level is rising, meditate on this image.
- Zero in on deep breathing. Although that's easy to overlook, research proves that it does relieve stress.

God comes to us in peace so a peaceful composure is the first step toward making thoughtful, God-centered decisions. It also brings peace to those around us.

In returning and rest you shall be saved; in quietness and in trust shall be your strength. (Isaiah 30:15)

Please, Lord, make me a channel of Your peace.

Through the Eyes of a Child

Ever notice how virtually everything is a source of awe and wonder for a young child?

The next time you have the opportunity, watch a young child watch snow falling. Or, notice the looks on the faces of little children when you drop Halloween candy in their baskets. For the little ones, the ordinary is fascinating and amazing.

If only we adults could retain that wonderment and awe! As everyday business takes over, where can we find true inspiration or just admiration?

The fact is, we are surrounded by miracles! Take a moment to really notice nature. Admire the intricate architecture of buildings you pass every day and previously failed to notice.

We can't regain the innocence of little children, but we can emulate their appreciation for the world's beauty and wonder.

The stars shone in their watches, and were glad...They shone with gladness for Him who made them. (Baruch 3:34)

Thank You, Creator, for human love; for sunrise and sunsets, moonrise and stars; for birdsong, sun and rain; for colors and smells; for all Your gifts.

Praying for Peace

"One of the greatest weapons against war, violence, hatred and racism is prayer," according to the National Black Catholic Evangelization Forum's Project Reach Out.

It points out that all Christians "need to embody a counter-cultural message of peace and non-violence and become more active in creating a culture of respect and reverence for life.

"This can be done by taking time each day to pray for a greater respect for life, for people everywhere regardless of their cultures and belief systems, for the environment, for universal peace and justice."

The world is crying out for love, mutual respect, wisdom and prudence even as it is engulfed in hatred, mistrust, ignorance, fear and violence.

How can you contribute to a culture that reveres all life?

Pay to all what is due them...respect to whom respect is due, honor to whom honor is due. (Romans 13:7)

Forgive us, Father, for the times we have turned our backs on love and compassion. Help us be peacemakers.

Very Special Love Letters

Andy Bremner was diagnosed with cancer at age eight. Over the next four years, his mother tried to cheer him by sending him letters from an anonymous friend.

After the death of her son, Linda Bremner remembered how much pleasure he had gotten from the mail. So she decided to write to the youngsters who went to a summer camp for those with cancer that Andy had attended. They loved her notes.

One child wrote, "Thank you, thank you, thank you for writing, I didn't think anyone knew I lived."

That was the beginning of Love Letters, a volunteer organization that sends cards, letters and gifts to more than 1200 sick children, many with rare or terminal diseases.

The pain of illness and the pain of grief can both be softened by love. Make an effort to reach out to someone who could benefit from your compassion.

Moved with compassion, Jesus touched their eyes. (Matthew 20:34)

Christ, help me use my life's difficulties, not as a cause of complaint, but an opportunity to assist others.

Building for the Future

Raúl Pastor was the winner of the National Humanitarian Architect Award of 2002 from Argentina's Society of Architects.

One cold day, Pastor, ten years an architect and a former teaching assistant at the University of Córdoba, who had been unemployed two years, heard a radio interview. He learned that Pedro Veras, his wife and two children were living in a tent because they couldn't pay rent.

He got authorization from the architects association to work pro-bono. Then he helped the Veras family build their own home. Since then, Pastor has helped more than 19 other families build their own homes through a project called "Las Hormigas" (the ants).

Pastor draws the house plans, teaches construction skills, does the paperwork to buy the land and gets recycled construction material. Raúl Pastor has turned his own despair and others' into hope–a model for everyone.

Someone needs what you have to give.

I have no silver or gold, but what I have I give you. (Acts 3:6)

Jesus, carpenter of Nazareth, inspire professionals to use their skills for the good of the neediest among us.

Sacred Beams

When New York City's World Trade Center collapsed into a mass of twisted beams, Rev. James Moore's Sacred Heart Parish in Albuquerque, New Mexico, was raising money for a tower to house a rediscovered parish bell.

John Garcia, a former official with the area's community development corporation, read that countries overseas were planning to recycle some of the steel from the World Trade Center.

So Rev. Moore and Mr. Garcia worked every connection they had, until finally, the office of the mayor in New York said they could have two beams for the bell tower, as long as they picked them up within five days.

They made the cross-country trip–and the deadline. And now those two beams are part of a new bell tower, calling people to life and hope.

God brings good out of evil if we allow it.

Do not let my treacherous enemies rejoice over me. (Psalm 35:19)

Master of all, Thank You for Your inspirations.

Family Matters

In 2003, *Family Circle* magazine reported on a national survey of American families. That study mentioned simple things families can do to keep strong, happy and hopeful in good times and in bad.

- Togetherness counts whether it's playing, praying, reading, weeding, even watching TV. Happy families invest in family life.

- Live by the Golden Rule – be nice to one another, love each other for no better reason than because you are family.

- The more bonds to family, friends and community, the better. Healthy families have a wealth of supportive relationships.

- Saving even a little regularly can have big benefits including hope against hard times.

- Strong families believe. Faith gets families through the tough times.

Do all you can to nurture your own happy, healthy family.

**Ascribe to the Lord, O families of the people, ascribe to the Lord glory and strength.
(1 Chronicles 16:28)**

Father, bless our nation and our world with healthy families.

Hide Your Kittens!

Many people complain about politicians. It's likely even more people would do so, if they knew that at least some politicians were kitten-eating space aliens.

That charge was made in an Ontario election in 2003, when one candidate issued a press release accusing another of being, "an evil reptilian kitten-eater from another planet."

Although the terrestrial candidate later admitted that the charge was "over the top," he refused to apologize. This unusual mud-slinging is an extreme form of the behavior that often, *ahem*, alienates many voters.

Yet as a responsible citizen, you don't have to just tolerate it. There are many ways you can get involved with local and national politics: write letters, sign petitions, attend rallies, e-mail your representatives, even get on the ballot for a local office.

Get involved. Be heard. Don't leave government to "space aliens."

By the blessing of the upright a city is exalted, but it is overthrown by the mouth of the wicked. (Proverbs 11:11)

Lord, help us to take responsibility for our communities.

Role Models—Who Needs Them?

How important are role models? Consider pro golfer Tiger Woods' impact on countless young aspiring golfers, particularly African Americans. His success has inspired many young people to take a new interest in the sport.

But while Woods certainly deserves credit, it was Earl Woods, his father, who invested the time, effort and patience needed to help his son hone his craft and skill on the golf course.

Charlie Sifford, the first black golfer to receive full membership in the Professional Golfers Association, emphasizes the importance of role models and mentors. "Tiger's father helped him along and his mother, too. ...You don't find parents today that take as much time to do this," he acknowledges.

Children aren't the only ones inspired by role models. Adults, too, need help, mentoring and guidance in pursuit of a goal. How can your talents, experience and hope help another?

Help my unbelief! (Mark 9:24)

Christ, remind me that I can find strength in asking for help when I need it. Make me aware of all the sources around me, too.

Why Vote?

Have you ever heard someone say that "you can't fight city hall?" Maybe, you've even thought this yourself. But if history can teach us anything, it's that the greatest problems of many nations have arisen from public apathy.

When people as a whole withdraw from the political arena, groups can monopolize the government unchecked by the best interests of citizens. Exercising your franchise (your right to vote) is essential to good government.

To make comparisons, if you want to get rid of weeds in a garden, plant something in their place; to get rid of darkness, turn on a light.

Similarly, if you want good government–and the overwhelming majority of people do–then you must work to elect people with sincere and honest ideals.

Democracy demands our participation. If we want good government, we have to make our voices heard and vote.

The Lord has...sent me to bring good news to the oppressed, to bind up the brokenhearted, to proclaim liberty to the captives. (Isaiah 61:1)

Author of our liberty, remind us to vote in every election.

Empty Spaces

Big cars, villas and private planes are the domain of the rich. But one rock star has asked this question: How much stuff do we really need?

"It seemed obscene of us to be rattling around in such a large home when others had nowhere to live," said legendary Pink Floyd guitarist David Gilmour.

Gilmour sold his London mansion for $5.2 million and donated every penny to Crisis, a housing charity, for a project aimed at creating a community of affordable housing and social services for London's homeless.

"It's an inspiring idea," Gilmour said. "It would be lovely to persuade a few more in my lucky position to do the same thing."

Even if we're not in a "lucky position," there is still a great deal we can do. There are a million ways to make a difference, and you don't need millions of dollars to do it.

Give alms from your possessions. (Tobit 4:7)

Father, my hands are Your hands on this earth. Infuse them with compassion and mercy.

Go Apart: Rest, Relax

Amidst the national crisis of the Civil War, President Lincoln found sanctuary not in the White House but further up Pennsylvania Avenue, in the Soldiers' Home.

After their son Willie died of typhoid fever in 1862, to help his grieving wife Mary as well as himself, President Lincoln moved his family to a cottage on the grounds of the Soldiers' Home, a few miles north of the White House. They spent the next three summers there. It's also where he slept the night before that fatal evening at Ford's Theater.

During those times of turmoil, President Lincoln was in search of a wartime retreat–to relax and clear his mind of the massive responsibilities weighing him down.

Have you taken time for yourself and your loved ones lately? At home or away, all of us need a respite from the cares of the day.

Come away to a deserted place all by yourselves and rest a while. (Mark 6:31)

Time is precious, Lord, but may we always make time to stop and notice Your presence in our lives.

An Inspiring Leader

Few except his fellow prisoners of war, knew what an inspiring leader Special Forces Captain "Rocky" Versace had been. But they wouldn't forget.

Versace was captured by the Viet Cong in 1963. For two years he maintained his leadership role, organizing, as the Associated Press reported, whatever resistance was possible under the circumstances: attempting escapes and repeatedly haranguing their captors.

According to the AP, "For his efforts, he suffered torture, solitary confinement, and medical neglect. He was last heard in 1965, just before he was executed, singing *God Bless America* while locked in an isolation box."

The surviving POWs nominated Versace for the Medal of Honor but not until the winter of 2001 was his valor officially acknowledged.

Valor, courage, is needed not just in extraordinary circumstances but in every day living. Pray for courage daily.

Be courageous and grow strong.
(1 Maccabees 2:64)

Prince of Peace, guide our leaders, guide all of us, in welcoming Your grace and seeking Your will in all we do.

A Centenarian's Recipe for Good Living

Giovanna Romanelli, Jenny to her friends, has a secret about how to live a long life. Her recipe isn't so mysterious, really, just full of common sense.

Every morning, she walks six blocks to church and then shops for dinner before returning home. As for medications, she says she takes "broccoli rabe, escarole, fresh fruit, pasta, white wine and the rosary."

Giovanna Romanelli has spent almost 60 years in the United States, since her husband brought her and their four children from Italy to New York after World War II. During these years she has been widowed and lost a son but gained 13 grandchildren, 32 great-grandchildren and two great-great-grandchildren. She says, "Hard work, good food, good family and the good Lord makes you live to be 100."

That's a healthy recipe for a happy life, however long it proves to be.

The human body is a fleeting thing, but a virtuous name will never be blotted out. (Sirach 41:11)

Under Your guidance, Blessed Trinity, all things are possible.

Answering a "Mob" Mentality

An angry mob, incensed over controversial observations in a history book about an Indian warrior-king, destroyed 30,000 ancient manuscripts at the Bhandarkar Oriental Research Institute (BORI) during a riot in India in 2004. Among the invaluable objects lost was an Assyrian clay tablet dated to 600 BC.

There was no way to retrieve the lost manuscripts, but within days a voluntary assistance group formed to help rebuild BORI. University students swept up glass and cleared debris. Analysts salvaged lost data from damaged computers. State offices and local businesses offered free supplies or labor. Said a volunteer: "I will help in any way I can, even...sweeping."

By coming together for good, the BORI volunteers were able to counteract the destruction caused by the mob.

Even the smallest, most seemingly insignificant actions can play a part in repairing great damage.

While God has overlooked the times of human ignorance, now he commands all people...to repent. (Acts 17:30)

Holy Lord, help us to do our part for good.

Making Music Together

The band Los Lobos has been making music together for about 30 years. Their experiences seem to echo those of any close relationship of long-standing.

"We were friends before we ever played music together," said Louie Perez, drummer and guitarist for the Grammy winning group. "We didn't join a band because someone placed a classified ad looking for musicians."

The group catapulted to commercial success with the release of *La Bamba,* a movie about the late Richie Valens, which featured eight Los Lobos performances.

They had to struggle to maintain their creative equilibrium amidst the fame, and the sorrows, such as the murder of the wife of guitarist Cesar Rosas. But they have also shared success.

Conrad Lozano, another performer in the 5-man band, hopes they can remain together for years to come. "That's the best thing we could do–keep it together as a group."

Every good relationship demands determination.

To the sound of musicians...they repeat the triumphs of the Lord. (Judges 5:11)

God, help us keep our most significant relationships in tune.

Something Unique

In the fast paced 21st century there is no time to stop and appreciate a still-operating 19th century power plant. Or is there?

Hidden in the bowels of Brooklyn's Pratt Institute is a boiler room like no other. It is presided over by the college's chief engineer, Conrad Milster.

He oversees what the *New York Times* called "an uncommon intersection of art and technology: ...a heady, hangarlike space dating to 1887, complete with spinning silver flywheels, incandescent dials, fuming pipes and century-old pistons."

At any time over the decades, someone could have justified gathering Pratt's old equipment for scrap metal or replacing it with diesel engines. Fortunately, some people appreciate the beauty of old machinery. An engineer says, "The wood, the tile–the complete fabric of that room is unique."

Celebrate your God-given individuality.

No one after drinking old wine desires new wine, but says, 'The old is good'. (Luke 5:39)

May we always acknowledge one another's individuality, Father, and appreciate what makes us each unique.

Age-Appropriate or Out of the Question?

Perhaps the only thing that has rivaled the incredible success of the *Harry Potter* book series is the debate about how suitable they are for young children.

Fans and critics continue to disagree on whether or not the books are appropriate for youngsters, given the storyline's focus on witchcraft and magic, and, in some cases, violence.

The series' author, J. K. Rowling, understands the sentiments behind the controversy. She admits, "I have never said these books are for very young children." Yet, she supports exposing children to the realities of evil in the world.

Examples like this reinforce the importance of the involvement of concerned adults in children's lives. Their well-being depends upon the actions, decisions and loving vigilance of parents, relatives, teachers, neighbors, coaches, spiritual and community leaders. Do your part for children, for the future.

**Children, be true to your training.
(Sirach 41:14)**

Jesus, I pray for the safety and serenity of all children.

More than a Pauper's Grave

Some stories just get to us. That's what happened when businessman David Bolger read a newspaper article about the death of a homeless man.

Marcos Melendez-Baires had moved from El Salvador to New Jersey in the early 1990's and worked there as a laborer. He became an alcoholic, finally losing all contact with his family, and ending up living–and dying–in a disabled truck.

But Bolger, a real estate company owner was determined to see that, at last, Melendez-Baires went home. He got official permission to have the body cremated after a religious service. Then he sent the ashes to the grateful family in El Salvador.

How does Bolger explain his concern for someone he never knew? "Just helping out a fellow human being," he says.

It's true that we can't help everybody. But we can make a real difference to some neighbors each day, whether we know them or not.

Assist your neighbor to the best of your ability. (Sirach 29:20)

Spirit of Love, show me how to be a good neighbor today.

Mommy, Daddy, and Then Toys

When psychiatrist Dr. Edward Hallowell asked his eight-year-old son what made him happy, he got a short answer: "Stuff."

Hallowell's five-year-old son, Tucker, however, was more articulate. First were "Mommy and Daddy," followed quickly by toys, trampolines, ice cream, candy, and hugs.

Sure, little Tucker came up with some standard answers. But his heart and mind went first to his parents, the two people who are devoted to ensuring his well-being.

Who looks to you for security and happiness? A child, a parent, a spouse; a friend in need or a relative? Whether or not they can articulate it, in your heart of hearts you know who is counting on you. Be there for them today.

He will gather the lambs in his arms, and carry them in His bosom, and gently lead the mother sheep. (Isaiah 40:11)

Good Shepherd, may I imitate Your loving care by responding to the needs of those around me.

The Seven "Ups"

Many of us play a daily waiting game—waiting for something to go wrong or right that will either break or make our day.

There really isn't any secret to having a positive outlook, but these seven "ups" are a good first step toward a fine day.

Wake Up! Decide to have a good day.

Dress Up! The best way to dress up is to put on a smile.

Shut Up! God gave us two ears and one mouth; try to do twice as much listening as talking.

Stand Up! Stand for something or you might fall for anything.

Look Up! …To the Lord.

Reach Up! …For something higher.

Lift Up! …Your prayers.

Want to make the world a better place? Positive, constructive action is essential and there's no better place to start than with our own attitudes.

Faith by itself, if it has no works, is dead. (James 2:17)

Father, You have blessed us with life. Help us to use it well, each day, each hour, each moment.

Fill Her Up, Please!

Chris Tombaugh was running out of gas. The director of a transitional housing facility for women had spent a busy afternoon at the office while waiting for Liddy, a client who wanted to return. Liddy, who struggled mightily with her addictions, insisted she wanted to get her life back on track.

But after waiting an extra two hours, Tombaugh had to leave for an appointment on the other side of town. The trouble was, her car was running on fumes. Nearing her destination, she passed a gas station. All eight pumps were out of gas. Finally, she saw two stations ahead. She chose the one on the left.

And there at that gas station stood Liddy, trying to find someone who would give her money for drugs. Relieved, she got in the car with Tombaugh.

Says the director: "There's not a doubt in my mind the Lord brought me there."

The Lord brings us many places, we just have to see it.

Admonish the idlers, encourage the faint hearted, help the weak. (1 Thessalonians 5:14)

Divine Physician, give Your healing to addicts.

Reaching Out With One's Heart

When Fidel Castro came to power, Ari Rodriguez and her family fled to Mexico.

While Rodriguez eventually left to go to the United States and become a citizen she hoped to repay the Mexican people for their kindness. In 1985, she helped establish an outreach program for Mexican and other migrant workers in Gainesville, Florida.

"I know how it feels to get here with no clothes, no shoes, no hope," she said. Rodriguez provides them with food, clothing, medical care and education. She says: "I love these people. When you love somebody, you want to always be there for them."

Have you showed someone–family member or stranger–that you love them today? Have you shown gratitude to God–through His people–for all your blessings?

Let us love one another, because love is from God. (1 John 4:7)

Loving Redeemer, help me share Your love with others. Help me share myself with others.

Hitting the Right Note

When you think of Grammy winners how often do you think of elementary school teachers?

"I was so euphoric, I didn't even hear my name," said Betty Scott who was a co-winner of the 1999 Grammy for best choral performance of Benjamin Britten's *War Requiem*. The Maryland Boy Choir, which she directed, was one of the groups participating. The choir included ten of her students at University Park Elementary School.

"To me the Grammy was an award for 34 years of teaching," said the Maryland educator. Scott is credited with helping develop an accomplished music program despite limited financial resources.

"There are days when I want to scream," said Scott. "But my unadulterated love for what I do is why I stayed."

Encourage the teachers you know—and don't forget to say, "Thanks."

Wisdom teaches her children. (Sirach 4:11)

Guide teachers, Jesus, and guard them from harm.

Thank God, There's a Nurse in the House

Kathy Copak listens to grieving people, talks with others about forgiveness, organizes support groups. She also takes blood pressure, gives flu shots and conducts basic medical exams.

Copak does all these things as a visiting nurse to homebound patients for her parish in Northwest Indiana. This wife, mother and grandmother worked in religious education before fulfilling her dream of becoming a nurse. After a stint in hospital nursing and home health care, she found the perfect match in the parish nurse program.

Copak prays with all the people she sees, finding it amazing that, no matter what, they always pray for someone else. She finds that healing comes just as much through "listening to people—to what's going on in their hearts, their struggles. ...It's wonderful to be part of this."

Make an effort to assist someone who is sick or in need of special attention. It could do you both good.

Do not hesitate to visit the sick. (Sirach 7:35)

When I am weary, Abba, lead me to rest; refresh me.

What God Won't Ask—and What He Will

When you come face to face with God, He won't ask about:

- the color of your skin
- the neighborhood where you lived, or the size of your house
- the clothes in your closets
- the money you made or your job title
- the popularity you experienced

But God will ask if you made your love for Him, for others, and for yourself, the measure of your life and deeds. God will also ask about:

- the content of your character
- the people you welcomed into your home
- the people you helped clothe and feed
- the chance that you compromised morality for position or wealth.
- the way you treated your neighbors

Love brought God to the Manger, the Upper Room, the Cross and His Ascension. Where has love brought you?

If I...do not have love, I am nothing.
(1 Corinthians 13:2)

Redeemer, thank You for making love the measure of Your life and deeds.

Fostering Tolerance

An African-American surgical technician and a white orthopedic surgeon shared a common concern about their Staten Island, New York, neighborhood. It was polarized.

So Jacob Carey and Dr. Mark Sherman organized the Unity Games, allowing 150 boys and girls of both races to play basketball and get past their differences.

Tysean Moore, 12, who is black, had fun during the weekend event, noting that he was glad to make new friends. "It's bringing a lot of people together," he said.

As Sally Ling, who is white, watched her daughter Rachel, 13, play ball, she said that children often do not learn enough about people of other races. "Another four years and she'll be in college," Ling observed. "It's a big world out there."

Two men with one thing in mind: getting people together to foster tolerance and mutual respect.

The commandments...are summed up in..."Love your neighbor as yourself." (Romans 13:9)

Creator, thank You, for the wondrous variety and beauty of human kind.

Climb Every Mountain

Some people didn't think that Erik Weihenmayer should try to climb the world's tallest mountain, Mount Everest. He heard those who urged caution, but neither listened to them nor saw them.

Weihenmayer, a well-trained and conditioned athlete, is blind. Born with a degenerative eye disease that led to loss of vision by his teens, his family supported but didn't pity him. When his parents and siblings went hiking he was expected to join them. He was a champion wrestler in high school and discovered climbing while in college.

As a mountaineer and a man who faces challenges and overcomes obstacles he had clear vision. Ultimately, Weihenmayer met the challenge of Everest along with team members who supported his quest, and was able to return safely to his wife and child. But if he faces another mountain, in nature or his personal life, he's ready to climb.

Conquer your own mountains, whatever they may be.

God, the Lord, is my strength; He makes my feet like the feet of a deer, and makes me tread upon the heights. (Habakkuk 3:19)

Adoni, close the ears of those with physical limitations to discouraging criticisms.

De-Stressing

Thanksgiving. Hanukkah. Christmas. Kwanzaa. All these holidays, and others, can equal STRESS.

Or you can learn to take out the stress. How?

- Remember God. Pray. Observe each holiday's religious traditions.
- Schedule free time for yourself.
- Limit visiting rather than trying to go to two or more homes on every holiday.
- Share holiday hosting with others. Don't try to do it all yourself.
- Give homemade gifts or paid certificates to such events as plays, massages, concerts, dance classes during the year.
- Shop for presents year round, not just before the holiday.

Holidays are meant to be enjoyable times, not endurance tests. Decide now to slow down. Refuse to over-commit. And, enjoy yourself.

There was a wedding in Cana...Jesus and His disciples had also been invited...Jesus said... "Fill the jars with water." (John 2:1,7)

Jesus, guest at a wedding party in Cana, help us really enjoy our holidays and parties.

Just Dessert

Stephen Gould and his family coordinated a neighborhood effort in the aftermath of the World Trade Center bombing. Collecting basic necessities including face masks and hard hats, they delivered them directly to Ground Zero workers.

On their way to the site one day, the chef at a local restaurant gave Gould a bag with twelve portions of apple brown Betty, still warm from the oven, saying, "Please give them to the rescue workers."

Finding the gesture kind, but not particularly useful, Gould agreed to make the delivery. He soon discovered he could not have been more wrong: the desserts went like the proverbial hot-cakes. "We gave the last one to a firefighter sitting alone in utter exhaustion," Gould said.

"Thank you," the man said, a twinkle in his eyes. "This is the most lovely thing I've seen in four days – and still warm!"

Do to others as you would have them do to you. (Luke 6:31)

Keep me open, loving God, to the many ways in which Your graces are shared.

World Wide School?

Andrew Chance was born with a congenital foot defect that required surgery and six weeks of recovery right at the start of the school year. Yet, though he wasn't able to get to St. Patrick's School in St. Joseph, Missouri, for weeks, the seventh grader missed hardly any school.

Using faxes, speaker phones, web cams and Internet uplinks, Andrew's mother and his teacher were able to hook Andrew up to his classroom digitally. A speaker cell phone and free minutes donated by Cingular Wireless even allowed Andrew to keep up-to-date on the goings-on of his math class, taught down the hall. It's not the same as being there, but it's the next best thing.

Creative solutions can be found for even the most vexing of problems. Learn to lean on ingenuity, not despair, when trouble arises.

You who fear the Lord, hope for good things, for lasting joy and mercy. (Sirach 2:9)

Spirit of Wisdom, help us to help others, and ourselves.

Bugged by Buzzards

One morning they were just there: Vultures, hundreds of them, sitting in pine trees near the center of Radford, Virginia.

Since that November morning in 2002, Radford and its outlying areas have been dealing with a problem that's afflicted many suburban, and even urban, areas. As development and expansion moves outwards into rural lands, people are being forced to deal with animals native to those areas or relocating into more populated territories.

In the case of Radford, residents have tried scaring the vultures away, and even killing them. The vultures persist, however, spreading a carrion smell throughout their roosts, damaging property and attacking the livestock of local farmers. Controversy abounds over the proper way of dealing with the vultures, or if it's even humane to do anything at all.

All of God's creatures affect the world around them, we human beings most of all. We human beings must always remember the responsibility we hold in regard to animals and nature as well as each other.

You are the salt of the earth. (Matthew 5:13)

Lord, help us to appreciate all of life's twists and turns.

Simplify Your Holidays

Holidays and holy days should mean peace, happiness, joy for the whole family. But what can you do when there's so much to do? Try these shortcuts to a happier time for all:

- Encourage youngsters' good deeds through an Advent calendar that suggests ways they can help others.

- When the tree is decorated, the menorah lit or the Kwanzaa decorations set up, gather as a family to read holiday literature, sing and play games.

- Reconnect with loved ones but limit gatherings to a few folks at a time, not standing room only mob scenes.

- Simplify the holiday feast, using healthy convenience foods as much as possible.

- Celebrate a silent evening with your family.

Make a decision in your home to use well the time that can slip away all too easily. Enjoy your family and your faith that are at the core of the holidays and holy days.

Rejoice in the Lord always; again I will say it, Rejoice. (Philippians 4:4)

God, guide our holiday celebrations.

Changing the World with Music

Some say Sam Phillips changed the world through music.

Mention Elvis Presley, Roy Orbison and Johnny Cash and even people with just a passing knowledge of mid-20th century American music will recognize them. Relatively unknown though he "discovered" those musicians and others, Phillips was 80 when he died in 2003.

Phillips opened Sun Records as the Memphis Recording Service in 1950. According to the *New York Times,* he wanted to "promote the music of people who had nowhere else to make their voice heard; to remove barriers between black and white music and musicians."

Unable to help great black musicians break into the mass market, Phillips helped insure the mass market would hear their music. He did what he could.

Today, right now, what can you do to make the world more human and humane?

Learn to do good; seek justice, rescue the oppressed, defend the orphan, plead for the widow. (Isaiah 1:17)

Just Judge, help us to make the world a better place for all.

Helping Out the Neighborhood

Have you ever wanted to do something good for the area you live in?

You may never have heard of Irma Fleck, but the people of the South Bronx will probably never forget her name.

The daughter and wife of physicians, Fleck spent many of her 84 years trying to stop the decline of the South Bronx. She helped put abandoned buildings and parking lots to new uses.

She contributed to the arts, developing the Bronx Council on the Arts and the Bronx Museum. And with Jack Flanagan, she formed the Bronx Frontier Development Corporation to collect spoiled produce from the Hunts Point Markets for use as fertilizer in gardens on vacant lots.

"When I work at something, it's like my child," Irma Fleck once said.

Consider your neighborhood your child. Nurture it. The small changes you make may be huge in others' eyes.

With justice you shall judge your neighbor... you shall not profit by the blood of your neighbor...love your neighbor as yourself. (Leviticus 19:15,16,18)

Creator, help us to be the best of neighbors.

You Are Whom You're With

"In the end," says Bill O'Reilly, host of TV's O'Reilly Factor, "you are not what you eat. Rather, you are whom you associate with."

In his book, *Who's Looking Out for You*, the controversial O'Reilly cautions readers to walk briskly away from destructive people, seeking generous people instead.

O'Reilly says that if we embrace honest, caring, and strong people, we will accomplish many positive things. "If you go it alone, or book passage on the ship of fools," he says, "expect one of those fools to toss you over the side when the big waves come. ... But a good friend will last a lifetime. And that person will look out for you if you demonstrate that you are worth looking out for."

O'Reilly follows his own advice. He makes it a point to gather his closest friends for a vacation retreat every other year.

Invest in the quality of your friendships.

A friend loves at all times. (Proverbs 17:17)

Loving God, bless me with genuine friends. And bless my friends.

The Power of a Good Listener

Many people fail to write letters or e-mails that either offer praise or constructive criticism because they don't believe it will do any good.

But the founder of The Christophers, Rev. James Keller, M.M., knew that decision makers are more susceptible to public opinion than is generally realized and that a few good letters do influence them. All it takes is a few minutes and some confidence. These tried and true tips from Father Keller can help:

- write as if to a friend
- be constructive
- be specific
- be brief without being curt
- make your point, but don't repeat it
- be yourself, writing as you talk
- offer positive suggestions, not just complaints

Your letter can not only be good, it can do good.

Take courage. (Haggi 2:4)

Holy Spirit, may my words build up, not tear down.

Giving Trees for Christmas

Beautifully decorated evergreen trees are a Christmas tradition. Yet for families with financial difficulties, they are one more unaffordable thing.

That's why some Girl Scout troops have an annual Christmas tree service project. Barbara Wallace, one of the organizers for 70 New York troops explains that the girls decorate donated artificial trees and give them away to needy families – 350 in the last few years.

The families range from those who have lost everything in house fires, to a young single mother and her newborn, to a woman struggling with alcoholism, though she had been sober for a year.

"She said the Christmas tree she selected, which a Brownie troop had decorated with paper angels, would remind her of God's love and her renewed commitment to serve Him," said Wallace.

We are reminded of God's love in many ways, often, through the loving concern of others.

By the tender mercy of our God, the dawn from on high will break upon us...to guide our feet into the way of peace. (Luke 1:78,79)

Holy Child, show us how to show Your beautiful face to others, in all we do.

Street Calls

How does a doctor make a house call if potential patients have no homes? In 1992, Dr. James Withers, dressed in torn jeans, medical bag at the ready, started visiting Pittsburgh's alleys. Dr. Withers treated colds, broken arms, pregnancies and heart attacks.

That was the start of Operation Safety Net. Today, doctors, nurses and counselors, guided by formerly homeless people, patrol city streets in the United States and in Canada, bringing cures and care to the streets.

Dr. Mark Meyer, who has been active in the Pittsburgh operation since 1994, believes the program has gotten people's lives on track. "Once we show them it matters that they're alive and need health care and food like the rest of us, we often don't see them on the streets anymore," he says.

It looks as though these physicians have written the perfect prescription–loving kindness. We can all dispense it.

Honor physicians for their services. (Sirach 38:1)

Your love is the greatest healer, Divine Physician.

The Promise

When Roberto Gonzales and his young wife Dora were expecting their first child, Roberto was involved in a 60-mph head-on automobile crash. Not knowing what the future held for their lives, Dora and Roberto made a solemn vow to do something for God's glory if Roberto's life was spared.

It took nearly 30 years before the opportunity presented itself, but in 1999, Roberto Gonzales, who had become a full-time santero or saint-maker in Albuquerque, New Mexico, received the commission for an altar screen for St. Paul the Apostle Catholic Church in Kress, Texas. He also was given the job of painting the church's doors, pews, altar, sanctuary chairs, and statues.

Pilgrims who have visited the church say the artwork has lifted their burdens. "I'm not very good at talking to people about God," says the artist, "but I think I can show Him in my art."

How can your talents reveal God to others?

The gifts He gave were...to equip the saints for the work of ministry, for building up the body of Christ. (Ephesians 4:11,12)

How do You want to share Your message through me, Lord Christ?

The Right Time to Meddle

Do you pride yourself on minding your own business? Most of the time, it is laudable to let people get on with their lives, but there are situations when you need to speak up.

Certainly, issues of health and safety can't be ignored. Is a friend the victim of domestic violence? Is a child being physically, emotionally or sexually abused? Is someone depressed or suicidal? Professional help is vital. Get information from community agencies, your local hospital, police, library, or simply the telephone directory.

But if you see a problem rather than a crisis, you have to decide if your intervention is really needed. Be sure your goal is worthy before giving unsolicited advice. Don't let your words sound like an attack. Remember, you can't force people to change.

Kindness, good sense and a touch of humility will go a long way in offering helpful ideas and friendly support.

The righteous gives good advice to friends. (Proverbs 12:26)

Merciful Lord, grant me the wisdom and courage to speak up when it's truly necessary for the well-being of others.

Pass the Broccoli—and the Balance Sheet

One evening, Bruce Cameron, a columnist for *Time* magazine, served his family more than meat and potatoes for dinner. The meal included a healthy helping of family finances.

"I realized that if we were going to spend less than 100 per cent of my monthly salary I was going to need the assistance of my entire household," he said, writing of the experience. He printed and distributed an accounting of every nickel made and spent by the Cameron family, sparing no detail.

Things changed after that evening's meal. The kids no longer argued when they passed up pricey treats at the grocery store, and they chose to wear a sweater before raising the thermostat.

"It's information I wish I'd had when I graduated from high school," concludes Cameron.

Parents need to take family finances seriously. And educating children about these realities is a boon to all.

Who is the faithful and prudent manager?
(Luke 12:42)

You fill my life with good things, Spirit of Counsel. In gratitude, may I be a wise manager of Your gifts.

When Only the Best Will Do

"It's perfectly shaped, about 100 years old, with a character of its own, holding its branches nicely erect." That is how David Murbach describes what he looks for in a Christmas Tree. Not just any tree, mind you. He selects the nationally famous crowd-pleaser that soars over New York City's Rockefeller Center each December.

Murbach, who has tended to Rockefeller Center's planting for many years, isn't always looking for perfection. "You want a tree that's natural looking with lots of zigzags, nooks and crannies."

Sometimes only perfection or as near to it as we human beings can achieve will do. But most times, natural looking with more than a few zigs and zags will do just fine.

What are human beings that You are mindful of them...You have made them a little lower than God. (Psalm 8:4,5)

Help us, Jesus, to love others and to love ourselves as we are. That, after all, is how You love us.

Interfaith Efforts

Little did U.S. Army Colonel William Roy know that when an Afghan soldier guided his company through Afghanistan, Roy would be instrumental in getting lifesaving help for that soldier's daughter.

The Kabul teenager was near death from severe malnutrition, parasitic infestations and a heart blockage. With the cooperation of the Departments of State and Defense, Col. Roy contacted Rev. Brian Jordan of Manhattan. Rev. Jordan brought her to the U.S. for surgery at Schneider Children's Hospital.

"You have a Roman Catholic priest bringing over an Afghani child to a Jewish hospital," Jordan said. "Talk about interfaith efforts. Religion should not be a means of violence. It should be a way of bringing people together."

We of many different faiths and beliefs, must all work together if our world is to survive.

Help your neighbors when they are in need, no matter their beliefs or lack of them.

A man was going down from Jerusalem to Jericho, and...a Samaritan...was moved with pity. (Luke 10:30,33)

Holy Trinity, help us to be tolerant and understanding of others.

Sheltering the True Victims

When California police officer Sue Webber-Brown makes an illegal drug arrest, the suspects aren't at the forefront of her mind—their children are.

That's because Webber-Brown knows the suffering the illegal drug trade brings to children. She has also seen how police officers who concentrate on nabbing drug users and dealers often treat these children as an afterthought.

Webber-Brown has endorsed the formation of task forces and policing techniques which emphasized the children. "They are the true victims" of the illicit drug trade, she says.

"The real victory is breaking the cycle" of illegal drug use, and pulling kids out of that environment, she says.

Support your community's efforts against illegal drugs. You will be helping more than the drug users themselves.

The Lord created medicines out of the earth, and the sensible will not despise them. (Sirach 38:4)

Divine Physician may we use drugs only for the relief of pain and for curing or controlling illness. Help us not to abuse them or become addicted to them.

A Dream Come True

Can you make a dying child's dream's come true? The Phoenix, Arizona Fire Department more than did it for a 6-year-old who was dying of leukemia.

Told by Billy's mother that her son wanted to be a fireman when he grew up, one of the firefighters ordered a complete uniform for Billy and arranged for him to spend a day as a fireman.

Early in the morning, Billy, dressed in his fire uniform and hat sat on the back of the truck and helped steer it to the fire station. He ate with the firemen. He answered the calls, riding in the different engines, the paramedic's van and even the chief's car.

Billy lived three months more than expected.

At the end, Billy's mother asked a fireman to be with him. Instead, sirens screaming, lights flashing, ladder extended to Billy's open window, 16 firefighters climbed into Billy's room, hugged him, held him and told him they loved him.

Unless you change and become like children, you will never enter the kingdom of heaven. (Matthew 18:3)

Abba, bless those who care for terminally ill children with tender compassion for their patients.

Words, Words, Words

Did you hear about the headbanger who complained about his McJob to the former dotcommer while they swilled longnecks?

If any of the terms in the above sentence seem unusual, that might be because they're new. Words such as "headbanger" (fan of heavy metal music), "McJob" (low paying, dead-end job), "dotcommer" (someone with an internet-related job) and "longneck" (beer in a long-necked bottle) were only recently recognized by the Merriam-Webster Collegiate Dictionary.

The Collegiate Dictionary is revised about once a decade or so, although new words are added each year. "It is a reflection of society's changes," said John Morse, president and publisher at Webster.

Not everyone enjoys change, especially changes in language, but change is inevitable. Pray to be able to embrace change in your own life.

From morning to evening conditions change; all things move swiftly before the Lord. (Sirach 18:26)

Lord, help us to find good in the changes around us.

Therapy in Everyday Things

Here are some remarkable conclusions from recent studies.

- Some people with arthritis find relief and strength after dancing.

- Some Parkinson's patients show greater motor skill improvement with music therapy than with physical therapy.

- Some cancer patients feel less pain after participation in art courses.

- Some individuals who've suffered brain injuries recover lost motor skills while working in gardens.

- Caring for pets can help lower blood pressure, lift depression and soothe stress.

As the relationship between emotional and physical health becomes clearer, our daily activities become more valuable. Relaxing and enjoyable outlets may actually have a great effect on our health.

What recharges your batteries? Be sure to make time for it.

My heart is glad, and my soul rejoices; my body also rests secure. (Psalm 16:9)

Grant me grace, Creator, to appreciate the amazing connection of my soul, body and mind.

Jump Right In

For Dorothy King, 9 a.m. can sometimes feel a little too early for a swim. But while the 78-year old's body may hesitate, her soul jumps right in. King belongs to the Harlem Honeys and Bears Swim Club, whose members range in age from 51 to 81. They don't just swim, they compete.

The Honeys and Bears have won scores of medals at the Empire State Senior Games and set several records. However, for club president Lettice Graham, 81, there's something more to the group's dedication than these achievements.

"I like to think that we can inspire the younger generations by showing them that growing old doesn't mean you can't stay active," she said. "These are the best years of our lives. We aren't sitting around doing nothing."

Life is worth living at every age. Jump in, body and soul.

How attractive is sound judgment in the gray-haired, and...good counsel...wisdom...understanding and...rich experience. (Sirach 25:4,5,6)

Father, You have blessed us with life. May we live it to the fullest through You and for You.

Christmas Finds a Home

One Christmas Eve, Lola M. Autry and her cocker spaniel, Casey J., saw a "scrawny, white-haired bird dog...thin...exhausted" near her mailbox. "His tail wagged a constant, friendly greeting."

She decided that she just couldn't care for another stray and tried to shoo him away. The dog stood there looking at them. Autry and Casey J. returned home.

Later, when she went to feed Casey J., the other dog was watching from a distance. Autry didn't offer him food, thinking he'd go where others would care for him. Instead, Casey J. "walked straight to the big dog, wagged her tail a few times, then turned toward the house" with the bird dog following. Then Casey J. watched calmly as her guest ate all her food.

Lola Autry named her new dog "Christmas" and cared for him for his last three weeks of life.

All God's creatures can remind us of our Creator's voice. Listen!

The wolf shall live with the lamb, the leopard...with the kid, the calf and the lion and the fatling...the cow and the bear...their young shall lie down together. (Isaiah 11:6,7)

God, open our ears to hear You in one another as well as in all Your works.

Ending Family Grudges

It's part of most families at some time – that grudge that keeps relatives apart. Here are a few simple strategies to end the madness and help the healing begin.

Locate the source of the separation. People carry the feeling of resentment after they forget the insult.

Use a neutral party to put things back together.

Meet, don't rehash. Invite your relative to a public activity such as a sports event, craft show, play, but do not discuss the incident.

Sometimes admitting blame, even though you think you're innocent, is the only way to break the bitterness.

Make persistent, realistic, regular attempts to reconnect with birthday cards, notes and e-mails.

Families aren't meant to live in anger but to joyfully celebrate the love that keeps them together.

**The Lord hates...haughty eyes, a lying tongue, ...a heart that devises wicked plans, ...and one who sows discord in a family.
(Proverbs 6:16,17,18,19)**

Abba, remind us that in You we are brothers and sisters, united by Your love.

Spread the Love

Ikey Harris, chairperson of The Northland Christmas Store, believes in giving others a "dignified Christmas".

The Christmas Store, established in 1988, has been feeding needy families for years. Several of their warehouses are stocked with canned goods so poor families can literally shop for food, free of charge. When they receive cash donations, they use them to stock up on supplies.

Harris calls the process a "community effort." The Christmas Store's good deeds have affected others; students in nearby schools help collect food to donate. For the past several years, a local department store has donated part of its profits for the day after Thanksgiving.

Although Christmas is certainly a time for giving, it must not be the only time. Generosity and caring have no boundaries of season or time. Be generous and caring everyday.

The righteous are generous. (Psalm 37:21)

Savior, help each of us remember Christmas' true meanings.

One Letter to Santa

A few years ago, a Fort Wayne, Indiana, radio station held a holiday promotion in which youngsters were asked to send their "wish list" letters to Santa.

"Dear Santa Claus," wrote one third-grader, "My name is Amy. I am nine years old. I have a problem at school. Can you help me Santa? Kids laugh at me because of the way I walk and run and talk. I have cerebral palsy. I just want one day where no one laughs at me or makes fun of me."

The station manager thought her story needed to be told, so the local paper carried it—within days it had traveled the world. Not only did Amy get her wish, but she got cards, letters and gifts from hundreds of well-wishers. More than that, parents and teachers world-wide used her story to discuss teasing and the importance of respect.

Fulfill a wish—your own, or someone else's.

You shall not revile the deaf or put a stumbling block before the blind; you shall fear your God; I am the Lord. (Leviticus 19:14)

Holy Jesus, let Your hope and Your love live in me, for my welfare and that of all Your children.

Tales and Dreams

International bestselling author Neil Gaiman writes novels, comics, children's books and scripts as he sees fit. His online web journal garners tens of thousands of hits a day. It's no wonder, then, that he can draw immense crowds at his public appearances. In an interview, he was once asked to account for that devotion.

"I think [the fans] want to say 'thank you,'" Gaiman said. "Sometimes they don't even have a book [for him to autograph]. Sometimes they bring you presents, sometimes they burst into tears. One girl fainted. I think you've given them something and you took them somewhere they couldn't have gone on their own."

Gaiman uses his talent to touch people in a way that resonates strongly with them.

How can you use your God-given talent to enrich the world?

A man, going on a journey, summoned his slaves and entrusted...to one...five talents, to another two, to another one, to each according to his ability. (Matthew 25:14,15

Lord, help us to recognize our talents and use them to the fullest extent possible.

Precious Gifts

As a foster mother, Alicia Swartz gives children the precious gift of a home, however temporary. She's also received much in return.

Swartz tells of the time she received the best present anyone had ever given her. As with all those she took in, Swartz knew that the spirited three-year-old girl would one day leave her. Nevertheless, she grew quite fond of the child who in turn became quite attached to an old stuffed rabbit that Swartz owned.

When it came time for the little girl to be adopted, Swartz gave the child a special present to remember her by–the beloved rabbit. The exuberant child hugged Swartz, ran into her bedroom a last time, and emerged with a stuffed bunny of her own. "Here," the girl said, "This is so you won't forget me either."

Love God's children, for their sakes, and for your own.

Do not despise one of these little ones; for...their angels continually see the face of My Father in heaven. (Matthew 18:10)

Infant Savior, may we appreciate what precious gifts children are.

One Holy Night

There are many tales about "Silent Night," one of the world's most beloved Christmas hymns.

People say the organ in a village church in Oberndorf, Austria broke down, rendering it useless for Christmas mass because mice had gnawed holes in the leather bellows. Others say Rev. Joseph Mohr was preparing a homily when he was asked to baptize a newborn child. He was inspired to write the hymn during the quiet walk home on that snowy evening. Some credit the song's spread to a master organ builder who came to repair the organ and asked for a copy of the hymn.

Whatever its true history, the choir director at St. Nicholas and Rev. Mohr first sang "Silent Night" with guitar accompaniment at midnight mass, 1818. And the gentle carol has journeyed into the hearts and minds of people around the world.

Open your heart to all that is beautiful and holy.

To you is born this day in the city of David a Savior, who is the Messiah, the Lord. ...You will find a child wrapped in bands of cloth and lying in a manger. (Luke 2:11, 12)

Jesus, God's Son and Mary's, fill our hearts with joy and gratitude at Your coming among us.

On Corinthians and Christmas

In his first letter to the Corinthians, St. Paul writes about what love is—and isn't. One holiday season, Rev. Victor Seidel, S.T., shared an anonymous adaptation in his Christmas letter. Here's a portion:

"If I decorate my house perfectly with strands of twinkling lights, but do not show love to my family, I'm just another decorator. If I slave away in the kitchen, baking Christmas cookies and preparing gourmet meals, I'm just another cook.

"If I work at the soup kitchen and give all that I have to charity, but do not show love to my family, it profits me nothing. ...Love stops the cooking to hug the child. Love sets aside the decorating to kiss the spouse. Love doesn't give only to those who are able to give in return, but rejoices in giving to those who can't.

"...Love never fails. Video games will break; pearl necklaces will be lost; golf clubs will rust. But the gift of love will endure."

Now faith, hope, and love abide...and the greatest of these is love. (1 Corinthians 13:13)

Holy Lord, help me to live Your love, as I bear all things, believe all things, hope all things, endure all things.

Bringing Peace Through Music

When most of us think of the West Bank in Israel, we think of the wars and violence that have plagued the Middle East for years.

But Daniel Barenboim believes music can drown out the din of the bombs and bullets. Despite the danger and frequent lack of security, the famed conductor and pianist plays to crowds of Palestinian students in an effort to bring peace to his war-torn region.

"Each one of us has a responsibility to do what is right, and not to wait for others to do it," he says. "My way is music. Maybe in this way, in a very small way we are able to break down the hatred that is so much in this region."

How do you take risks for peace? There are countless ways to work toward peace, whether it involves volunteering your time, or speaking out against injustice.

**Lead a quiet and peaceable life.
(1 Timothy 2:2)**

Jesus, You set the perfect example of peacemaker. I ask the Holy Spirit for guidance in following You in this way.

Let Me Count the Ways

When Donna Gephart was diagnosed with cancer, she became overwhelmed by numbers.

"Six was the number that changed my life," she writes. "That was the size, in centimeters, of the tumor growing on my left ovary."

Seven was the number of days she'd be in the hospital each month for three months. Sixty-three became the number of times someone poked a needle into her.

But at some point, Gephart began to realize these weren't the really significant numbers.

"The most important number in my life was two," she said. That's how many sons she had. She also cherished twelve, the number of years she and her husband had been married when they came to understand the meaning of "in sickness and in health."

"The value of family and friends can't be measured," she observed. "The power of that kind of love extends to infinity."

Let love be genuine...love one another with mutual affection. (Romans 12:9,10)

When we are overwhelmed, Beloved Father, open our eyes to the goodness that surrounds us.

True Champions

In the euphoria of winning the state championship, no one bothered to look at the scorecard of Westborough High's golf team. It had been an extremely close match, but they had won the Massachusetts state title and were headed for a victory celebration.

On the bus, Coach Greg Rota began reviewing the scores, interested in seeing how each of his players had fared. To his dismay, he realized that the nine-stroke score one of his students had made had been inadvertently recorded as a seven.

The Boston Globe reported that Woburn High's Coach Bob Doran accepted the championship trophy with amazement. "No one would have known," he said.

As for Coach Rota, he never hesitated to do the right thing. His perspective on the situation was simple: "The trophy wasn't ours to take."

Honesty counts most when it's hard, not when it's easy.

Birds roost with their own kind, so honesty comes home to those who practice it. (Sirach 27:9)

Lord, remind us that You reward honesty.

Helping Hands

Holy Apostles Soup Kitchen in New York City has been praised by many of the people it serves. Begun in 1982, it served 350 meals a day. Now it supplies more than 1,000 meals a day. But in this case, the higher the number, the sadder the situation. Says volunteer Louraine Goodrich, "I just think it's terrible that people don't earn enough (to pay) for food."

Surprisingly, 40 per cent of the clients are employed but have difficulty meeting their expenses.

Noel Rodriguez lost his job and apartment after injuring his back, and eats lunch at the soup kitchen to save money. He says, "Here, they treat you with respect."

Another client, Eddie Brown, a messenger, says, "Coming here, it renews my faith in humanity."

It's good to know others are there to help us in times of need. Don't be afraid to accept assistance. And offer help when you are able.

To deprive an employee of wages is to shed blood. (Sirach 34:27)

Holy Spirit, thank You for the angels that walk among us.

Balancing Act

"The tragedy of human history lies in the enormous potential for destruction in rare acts of evil, not in the high frequency of evil people," wrote scientist Stephen Jay Gould. He called it "the Great Asymmetry," noting that every spectacular incident of evil will be balanced by l0,000 acts of often unnoted and invisible kindness.

In a culture that pays excessive attention to tragic, senseless, and sensational acts, it is easy to miss the goodness.

Pay attention to your surroundings. Revel in the energy found in an urban street's bustle or a minivan jam-packed with budding ballerinas. Make the effort to find and share the kindness in your life. Be gentle with family members, neighbors and colleagues. It's not difficult: just slow down and listen.

Make sure you contribute to those 10,000 acts of kindness.

Kindness is like a garden of blessings. (Sirach 40:17)

Keep our focus on all that is good, God of life and love.

Finding Joy in Service

"Happy Birthday." "Happy Thanksgiving." "Happy New Year." We often wish one another happiness. But wishing it and experiencing it are two different things.

John Mason Brown, a literary critic offers these thoughts on the subject of happiness:

"No one, I am convinced, can be happy who only lives for oneself. The joy of living comes from immersion in something that we know to be bigger, better, more enduring and worthier than we are. People, ideas, causes–these offer the one possible escape, not merely from selfishness but from the hungers of solitude and the sorrows of aimlessness.

"The only true happiness comes from squandering ourselves for a purpose."

Do you know your purpose in life? Does it include service to others? It's hard to imagine our hearts knowing happiness unless we try, with God's help, to help others know it, too.

The Son of Man came not to be served but to serve. (Mark 10:45)

Jesus Christ, Your life, Your death, Your resurrection were all for our sakes. Help me imitate You in serving my brothers and sisters with all my heart.

Also Available

Have you enjoyed volume 39 of *Three Minutes a Day?* These other Christopher offerings may interest you:

- **News Notes** – published ten times a year on a variety of topics of current interest. One copy as published is free; bulk and standing orders available.

- **Ecos Cristóforos** – Spanish translations of selected News Notes. Issued six times a year. One copy as published is free; bulk and standing orders available.

- **Wall or Desk Appointment Calendar and Monthly Planner** – The Calendar offers an inspirational message for each day. The Monthly Planner with its trim, practical design also offers a monthly inspirational message.

- **Videocassettes** – Christopher videos range from wholesome entertainment to serious discussions of family life and current social and spiritual issues.

For more information on The Christophers or to receive **News Notes, Ecos Cristóforos** or a catalogue:

> The Christophers
> 12 East 48th Street
> New York, NY 10017
>
> Phone: 212-759-4050
>
> E-mail: mail@christophers.org
>
> Web site: www.christophers.org

The Christophers is a non-profit media organization founded in 1945. We share the message of personal responsibility and service to God and humanity with people of all faiths and no particular faith. Gifts are welcome and tax-deductible. Our legal title for wills is The Christophers, Inc.